This Planner Belongs To:

NAME_____

PHONE_____

EMAIL_____

Broad Book Press, Publisher

Copyright © 2025 by Broad Book Group

All rights reserved.

No part of this publication may be reproduced, distributed, or transmitted in any form or by any means, including photocopying, recording, or other electronic or mechanical methods, without the prior written permission of the publisher, except in the case of brief quotations embodied in critical reviews and certain other noncommercial uses permitted by law. For permission requests, write to the publisher, subject line "Attention: Permissions" at info@broadbookgroup.com.

Paperback ISBN: 9781963549201

Published in the United States by Broad Book Press, an imprint of Broad Book Group, Edwardsville, IL.

Library of Congress Control Number: 2025903483

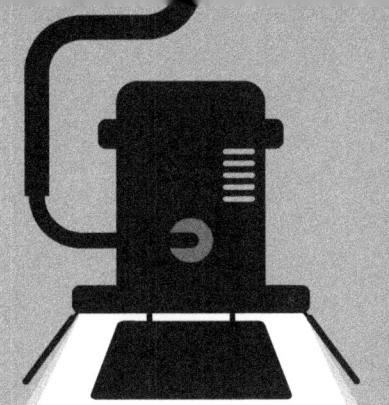

the ACTOR'S LIFE PLANNER

a 12-week planner

CORRIE LEGGE

broad book press

Introduction

WELCOME TO THE ACTOR'S LIFE PLANNER!

As an actor myself, I know the unpredictable cycle of auditions, rehearsals, day jobs, and personal commitments. It can feel nearly impossible to juggle pursuing a creative career while still having a personal life. I also know how challenging it can feel to stay consistent in an industry where no two days look the same.

That's why I created *The Actor's Life Planner*—the first planner designed for actors' ever-changing schedules. Unlike traditional planners, this one adapts to your creative process, helping you stay focused and flexible at the same time. Using my experience from years of coaching multi-passionate artists, I built this planner to help you stay on track—no matter how unpredictable life gets.

This planner will help you:

- **Design your dream creative life.** Visualize your dream life, and take intentional steps toward it with clarity and purpose.
- **Prioritize what truly matters.** Use regular self-reflection exercises to ensure you're prioritizing the goals and tasks that move you towards what you truly want.

- **Plan with purpose.** Customize your day using flexible 24-hour blocks, so you can visualize all your bookings, auditions, rehearsals, day job, and more.
- **Celebrate your wins.** From feeling truly connected in class to booking a series regular, recognize every win—big or small—and keep your momentum alive!
- **Stay flexible to opportunities.** Be ready for last-minute auditions and bursts of creative inspiration. With pages designed to fit your ever-changing needs, you can stay on track even when opportunities necessitate a pivot.
- **Capture your bursts of genius.** Keep all your ideas in one place so you never lose those flashes of brilliance.
- **Unlock exclusive resources.** Gain access to bonus training videos, prompts, and exercises to support your journey. Visit **ACTANDCREATIVES.COM/PLANNER-TOOLS** or scan the QR code to grab yours now.

You've already taken a huge step toward your dreams by choosing this planner. Now it's time to dive in and make it your own! Stay organized, track your wins, and enjoy the process. You've got this!

I can't wait to see what you create!

Corrie

Contents

HOW TO NAVIGATE THIS PLANNER 8
MY LIFE PIE 10
MY DREAM LIFE 13
MY FOCUS GOALS 15
MINI HABITS 22
12-WEEK OVERVIEW 24
CREATIVE ROUTINES 30
DREAM WEEK 32
ACTING WINS 34
MONTHLY PLANNER & REFLECTIONS 36
DAILY PLANNER 52
MY LIFE PIE NOW 232
MY 12-WEEK REFLECTION 236

HOW TO NAVIGATE THIS PLANNER

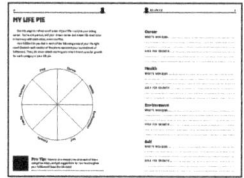

My Life Pie 10
Use this page to reflect on all areas of your life—not just your acting career. You'll shade in each section of the pie to represent your current level of fulfillment and jot down what's working and where there's area for growth for each category in your life pie.

My Dream Life 13
Outline and visualize your bigger dreams and aspirations however you're inspired to—collage images, doodle, write, create word art... the choice is yours. Focus on your broader life vision. Think big and imagine the life you want to create.

My Focus Goals 15
Choose goals that align with your vision for your dream life. Keep it simple and actionable. Which goals will have the biggest impact on your life as a whole? These are your key steps toward making that dream life a reality.

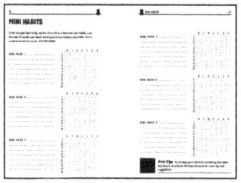

Mini Habits 22
Small changes lead to big results. Commit to a few new mini habits over the next 12 weeks and watch the impact of consistent, tiny shifts. Never underestimate the power of small steps!

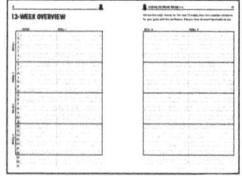

12-Week Overview 24
Map out your major events for each month and set milestones based on your focus goals.

HOW TO NAVIGATE THIS PLANNER

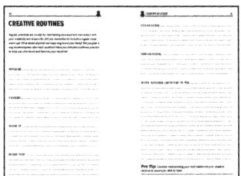

Creative Routines 30
Regular practices are crucial for maintaining structure and connection with your creativity and dream life. Use this space to build routines that keep you on track and inspired.

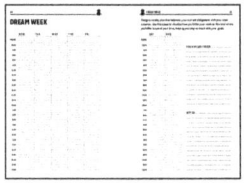

Dream Week 32
Design a weekly plan that balances your current obligations with your ideal schedule. Use this space to visualize how you'd like your week to flow and where you'd like to spend your time, helping you stay on track with your goals.

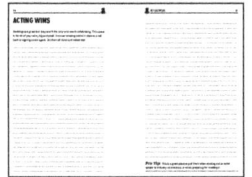

Acting Wins 34
Track all your wins, big and small. From an amazing scene in class to a callback or booking, jot them all down.

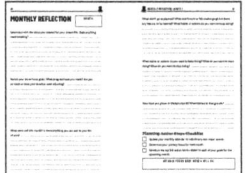

Monthly Reflections 38, 42, 46, 50
Reconnect with the vision you created for your dream life. Does anything need tweaking? Revisit your three focus goals. What progress have you made? Have you grown in the last month? What led to that growth?

Daily Planner 52
Plan for your days as they happen while keeping track of your main focus goals and your to-do tasks.

MY LIFE PIE

Use this page to reflect on all areas of your life—not just your acting career. You're one person, and your dream career and dream life need to be in harmony with each other, not in conflict.

How fulfilled do you feel in each of the following areas of your life right now? Shade in each section of the pie to represent your current level of fulfillment. Then, jot down what's working and where there's area for growth for each category in your life pie.

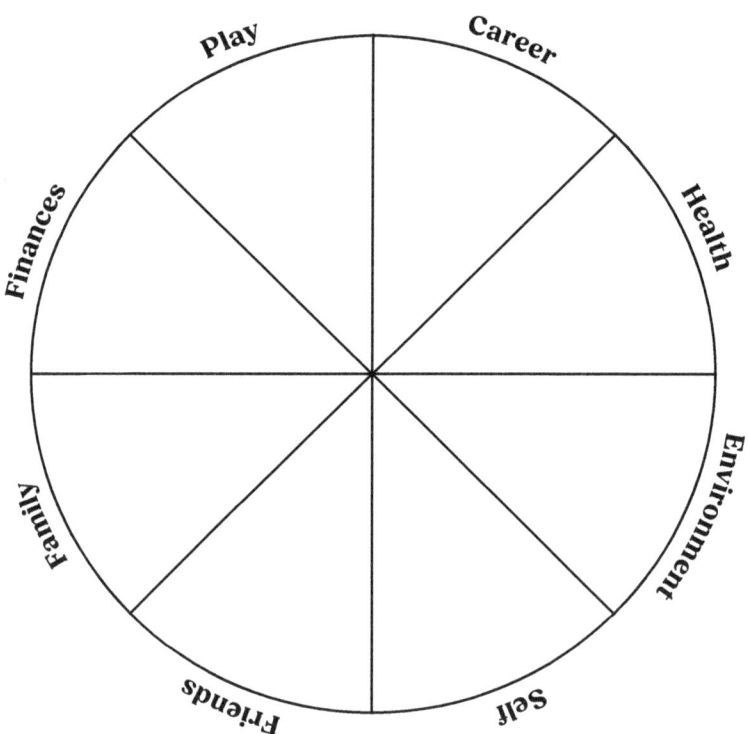

Pro Tip: Want to dive deeper into what each of these categories mean, and get suggestions for how to strengthen your fulfillment? Scan the QR code!

Career

WHAT'S WORKING ....
....
....

AREA FOR GROWTH ....
....
....

Health

WHAT'S WORKING ....
....
....

AREA FOR GROWTH ....
....
....

Environment

WHAT'S WORKING ....
....
....

AREA FOR GROWTH ....
....
....

Self

WHAT'S WORKING ....
....
....

AREA FOR GROWTH ....
....
....

Friends

WHAT'S WORKING ....
....
....

AREA FOR GROWTH ....
....
....

Family

WHAT'S WORKING ....
....
....

AREA FOR GROWTH ....
....
....

Finances

WHAT'S WORKING ....
....
....

AREA FOR GROWTH ....
....
....

Play

WHAT'S WORKING ....
....
....

AREA FOR GROWTH ....
....
....

MY DREAM LIFE

Use the next two pages to outline and visualize your bigger dreams and aspirations. Feel free to use it however inspires you—collage images, doodle, write, create word art... the choice is yours. Focus on your broader life vision. Think big and imagine the life you want to create. These pages will serve as a reminder of the dream life you're working towards during these 12 weeks.

Pro Tip: Check in with your dream life daily, so it's always top of mind.

MY DREAM LIFE

MY FOCUS GOALS

It's time to identify your top three focus goes for the next 12 weeks. Choose goals that align with your vision for your dream life. Keep it simple and actionable. Which goals will have the biggest impact on your life as a whole?

1. ....
....
....
....
....
....
....

2. ....
....
....
....
....
....
....

3. ....
....
....
....
....
....
....

Pro Tip: Scan code for additional exercises and guidance designed to help you set focus goals that are aligned with your dream life, so you can move towards that vision with clarity, joy, and intentional action.

MY FOCUS GOALS

MY FIRST FOCUS GOAL

....
....
....
....

This goal is important to me because: ....
....
....
....

Accomplishing this would change my life for the better by: ....
....
....
....

Some challenges I may face are: ....
....
....
....

Mini-habits I could start that would support this goal are: ....
....
....
....

I will celebrate achieving this goal by: ....
....
....
....

Brainstorm Steps

Action Plan

DATE	ACTION	✔

MY FOCUS GOALS

MY SECOND FOCUS GOAL

....
....
....
....

This goal is important to me because: ....
....
....
....

Accomplishing this would change my life for the better by: ....
....
....
....

Some challenges I may face are: ....
....
....
....

Mini-habits I could start that would support this goal are: ....
....
....
....

I will celebrate achieving this goal by: ....
....
....
....

Brainstorm Steps

Action Plan

DATE	ACTION	✔

MY THIRD FOCUS GOAL

....
....
....
....

This goal is important to me because: ....
....
....
....

Accomplishing this would change my life for the better by: ....
....
....
....

Some challenges I may face are: ....
....
....
....

Mini-habits I could start that would support this goal are: ....
....
....
....

I will celebrate achieving this goal by: ....
....
....
....

Brainstorm Steps

Action Plan

DATE	ACTION	✔

MINI HABITS

Small changes lead to big results. Commit to a few new mini habits over the next 12 weeks and watch the impact of consistent, tiny shifts. Never underestimate the power of small steps!

MINI HABIT 1 ....

....

....

....

....

....

....

	M	T	W	T	F	S	S
1							
2							
3							
4							
5							
6							
7							
8							
9							
10							
11							
12							

MINI HABIT 2 ....

....

....

....

....

....

....

	M	T	W	T	F	S	S
1							
2							
3							
4							
5							
6							
7							
8							
9							
10							
11							
12							

MINI HABIT 3 ....

....

....

....

....

....

....

	M	T	W	T	F	S	S
1							
2							
3							
4							
5							
6							
7							
8							
9							
10							
11							
12							

MINI HABIT 4 ....

....
....
....
....
....
....

	M	T	W	T	F	S	S
1							
2							
3							
4							
5							
6							
7							
8							
9							
10							
11							
12							

MINI HABIT 5 ....

....
....
....
....
....
....

	M	T	W	T	F	S	S
1							
2							
3							
4							
5							
6							
7							
8							
9							
10							
11							
12							

MINI HABIT 6 ....

....
....
....
....
....
....

	M	T	W	T	F	S	S
1							
2							
3							
4							
5							
6							
7							
8							
9							
10							
11							
12							

Pro Tip: Try to keep your habits to something that takes less than 5 minutes to do! Scan QR code for more tips and suggestions.

12-WEEK OVERVIEW: WEEKS 1-4

	MM/DD	EVENT	GOAL 1
WEEK 1			
WEEK 2			
WEEK 3			
WEEK 4			

12-WEEK OVERVIEW: WEEKS 1-4

List out the major events for the next 12 weeks, then set a realistic milestone for your goals with the confidence that you have time and bandwidth to act.

GOAL 2	GOAL 3

....
....

12-WEEK OVERVIEW: WEEKS 5-8

	MM/DD	EVENT	GOAL 1
WEEK 5			
WEEK 6			
WEEK 7			
WEEK 8			

GOAL 2	GOAL 3

12-WEEK OVERVIEW: WEEKS 9-12

	MM/DD	EVENT	GOAL 1
WEEK 9			
WEEK 10			
WEEK 11			
WEEK 12			

GOAL 2

GOAL 3

CREATIVE ROUTINES

Regular practices are crucial for maintaining structure and connection with your creativity and dream life.

Did you remember to include a regular vocal warm up? What about physical warmups to ground your body? Did you plan a way to decompress after each audition? Have you included a stillness practice to help you slow down and listen to your intuition?

MORNING..
....
....
....
....

EVENING..
....
....
....
....

WARM-UP..
....
....
....
....

SCENE PREP..
....
....
....
....

CREATIVE ROUTINES

PRE-AUDITION ....
....
....
....
....

POST-AUDITION ....
....
....
....
....

OTHER IMPORTANT ROUTINES ....
....
....
....
....
....
....
....
....
....
....
....
....
....
....

Pro Tip: Consider incorporating your mini habits into your creative routines to ensure you stick to them.

DREAM WEEK

	MON	TUE	WED	THU	FRI
THEME					
12:00					
1:00					
2:00					
3:00					
4:00					
5:00					
6:00					
7:00					
8:00					
9:00					
10:00					
11:00					
12:00					
1:00					
2:00					
3:00					
4:00					
5:00					
6:00					
7:00					
7:00					
8:00					
9:00					
10:00					
11:00					
12:00					

DREAM WEEK

33

Design a weekly plan that balances your current obligations with your ideal schedule. Use this space to visualize how you'd like your week to flow and where you'd like to spend your time, helping you stay on track with your goals.

	SAT	SUN
THEME		
12:00		
1:00		
2:00		
3:00		
4:00		
5:00		
6:00		
7:00		
8:00		
9:00		
10:00		
11:00		
12:00		
1:00		
2:00		
3:00		
4:00		
5:00		
6:00		
7:00		
7:00		
8:00		
9:00		
10:00		
11:00		
12:00		

RECURRING TASKS ....

....
....
....
....
....
....
....
....
....
....

NOTES ....

....
....
....
....
....
....
....
....
....

ACTING WINS

Bookings are great but they aren't the only wins worth celebrating. This space is for all of your wins, big and small. From an amazing scene in class to a callback or signing with a new agent. Jot them all down and celebrate!

....
....
....
....
....
....
....
....
....
....
....
....
....
....
....
....
....
....
....
....
....
....
....
....
....
....

ACTING WINS

Pro Tip: This is a great place to pull from when sending out an actor update to industry connections or when preparing for meetings!

MONTHLY PLANNER 1

MONTH:

MON	TUE	WED

MONTHLY PLANNER 1

MY MAIN FOCUS THIS MONTH WILL BE:

THU	FRI	SAT	SUN

MONTHLY REFLECTION

MONTH:

Reconnect with the vision you created for your dream life. Does anything need tweaking? ....
....
....
....
....
....
....
....

Revisit your three focus goals. What progress have you made? Are you on track or does your timeline need adjusting? ....
....
....
....
....
....
....
....

What went well this month? Is there anything you can add to your list of wins? ....
....
....
....
....
....
....
....

What didn't go as planned? What didn't work or felt challenging? Are there any lessons to be learned?...
....
....
....
....
....
....

What habits or actions do you want to keep doing? What do you want to start doing? What do you want to stop doing? ....
....
....
....
....
....
....
....

How have you grown in the last month? What has led to that growth? ....
....
....
....
....
....

Planning Action Steps Checklist

☐ Update your monthly calendar to include any new major events.

☐ Determine your primary focus for next month.

☐ Schedule the top 3-5 action items related to each of your goals for the upcoming month.

MY MAIN FOCUS NEXT MONTH WILL BE:

MONTHLY PLANNER 2

MONTH:

MON	TUE	WED

MONTHLY PLANNER 2

MY MAIN FOCUS THIS MONTH WILL BE:

THU	FRI	SAT	SUN

MONTHLY REFLECTION

MONTH:

Reconnect with the vision you created for your dream life. Does anything need tweaking? ....
....
....
....
....
....
....
....

Revisit your three focus goals. What progress have you made? Are you on track or does your timeline need adjusting? ....
....
....
....
....
....
....
....

What went well this month? Is there anything you can add to your list of wins? ....
....
....
....
....
....
....

What didn't go as planned? What didn't work or felt challenging? Are there any lessons to be learned?..
....
....
....
....
....
....

What habits or actions do you want to keep doing? What do you want to start doing? What do you want to stop doing? ....
....
....
....
....
....
....

How have you grown in the last month? What has led to that growth? ....
....
....
....
....
....

Planning Action Steps Checklist

- [ ] Update your monthly calendar to include any new major events.
- [ ] Determine your primary focus for next month.
- [ ] Schedule the top 3-5 action items related to each of your goals for the upcoming month.

MY MAIN FOCUS NEXT MONTH WILL BE:

MONTHLY PLANNER 3

MONTH:

MON	TUE	WED

MONTHLY PLANNER 3

MY MAIN FOCUS THIS MONTH WILL BE:

THU	FRI	SAT	SUN

MONTHLY REFLECTION

MONTH:

Reconnect with the vision you created for your dream life. Does anything need tweaking? ....
....
....
....
....
....
....
....

Revisit your three focus goals. What progress have you made? Are you on track or does your timeline need adjusting? ....
....
....
....
....
....
....
....

What went well this month? Is there anything you can add to your list of wins? ....
....
....
....
....
....
....
....

What didn't go as planned? What didn't work or felt challenging? Are there any lessons to be learned?..
....
....
....
....
....
....

What habits or actions do you want to keep doing? What do you want to start doing? What do you want to stop doing? ....
....
....
....
....
....
....
....

How have you grown in the last month? What has led to that growth? ....
....
....
....
....
....

Planning Action Steps Checklist

- [ ] Update your monthly calendar to include any new major events.
- [ ] Determine your primary focus for next month.
- [ ] Schedule the top 3-5 action items related to each of your goals for the upcoming month.

MY MAIN FOCUS NEXT MONTH WILL BE:

MONTHLY PLANNER 4

MONTH:

MON	TUE	WED

MONTHLY PLANNER 4

MY MAIN FOCUS THIS MONTH WILL BE:

THU	FRI	SAT	SUN

MONTHLY REFLECTION

MONTH:

Reconnect with the vision you created for your dream life. Does anything need tweaking? ....
....
....
....
....
....
....
....

Revisit your three focus goals. What progress have you made? Are you on track or does your timeline need adjusting? ....
....
....
....
....
....
....
....
....

What went well this month? Is there anything you can add to your list of wins? ....
....
....
....
....
....
....
....

What didn't go as planned? What didn't work or felt challenging? Are there any lessons to be learned? ....
....
....
....
....
....
....

What habits or actions do you want to keep doing? What do you want to start doing? What do you want to stop doing? ....
....
....
....
....
....
....

How have you grown in the last month? What has led to that growth? ....
....
....
....
....
....

Planning Action Steps Checklist

☐ Update your monthly calendar to include any new major events.

☐ Determine your primary focus for next month.

☐ Schedule the top 3-5 action items related to each of your goals for the upcoming month.

MY MAIN FOCUS NEXT MONTH WILL BE:

 **DAILY PLANNER**

TODAY'S DATE:

TODAY'S FOCUS:

Today's Events

- 12:00
- 1:00
- 2:00
- 3:00
- 4:00
- 5:00
- 6:00
- 7:00
- 8:00
- 9:00
- 10:00
- 11:00
- 12:00
- 1:00
- 2:00
- 3:00
- 4:00
- 5:00
- 6:00
- 7:00
- 8:00
- 9:00
- 10:00
- 11:00
- 12:00

CURRENT FOCUS GOALS

....
....
....
....
....
....

TIME LEFT FOR GOALS:

MUST DO

☐ ....
☐ ....
☐ ....

IF TIME

☐ ....
☐ ....
☐ ....

CREATIVE PLAY

....
....
....
....
....
....

DAILY PLANNER

RELATIONSHIPS NURTURED

....
....
....
....
....
....

TODAY'S POSITIVES

....
....
....
....
....
....

Notes

DAILY CHALLENGE
Find an upcoming networking event near you and add it to your calendar.

DAILY PLANNER

TODAY'S DATE:	TODAY'S FOCUS:

Today's Events

- 12:00
- 1:00
- 2:00
- 3:00
- 4:00
- 5:00
- 6:00
- 7:00
- 8:00
- 9:00
- 10:00
- 11:00
- 12:00
- 1:00
- 2:00
- 3:00
- 4:00
- 5:00
- 6:00
- 7:00
- 8:00
- 9:00
- 10:00
- 11:00
- 12:00

CURRENT FOCUS GOALS

....
....
....
....
....
....

TIME LEFT FOR GOALS:

MUST DO

☐ ....
☐ ....
☐ ....

IF TIME

☐ ....
☐ ....
☐ ....

CREATIVE PLAY

....
....
....
....
....
....

RELATIONSHIPS NURTURED

....
....
....
....
....
....

TODAY'S POSITIVES

....
....
....
....
....
....

Notes

DAILY CHALLENGE
Incorporate a **PLAYTAKE PROMPT** into your scene work today. Scan the QR code to learn more.

 **DAILY PLANNER**

| TODAY'S DATE: | TODAY'S FOCUS: |

Today's Events

- 12:00
- 1:00
- 2:00
- 3:00
- 4:00
- 5:00
- 6:00
- 7:00
- 8:00
- 9:00
- 10:00
- 11:00
- 12:00
- 1:00
- 2:00
- 3:00
- 4:00
- 5:00
- 6:00
- 7:00
- 8:00
- 9:00
- 10:00
- 11:00
- 12:00

CURRENT FOCUS GOALS

....
....
....
....
....
....

| TIME LEFT FOR GOALS: |

MUST DO

☐ ....
☐ ....
☐ ....

IF TIME

☐ ....
☐ ....
☐ ....

CREATIVE PLAY

....
....
....
....
....
....

RELATIONSHIPS NURTURED

....
....
....
....
....
....

TODAY'S POSITIVES

....
....
....
....
....
....

Notes

DAILY CHALLENGE
Create a character playlist or vision board for your dream role.

DAILY PLANNER

TODAY'S DATE:	TODAY'S FOCUS:

Today's Events

- 12:00
- 1:00
- 2:00
- 3:00
- 4:00
- 5:00
- 6:00
- 7:00
- 8:00
- 9:00
- 10:00
- 11:00
- 12:00
- 1:00
- 2:00
- 3:00
- 4:00
- 5:00
- 6:00
- 7:00
- 8:00
- 9:00
- 10:00
- 11:00
- 12:00

CURRENT FOCUS GOALS

....
....
....
....
....
....

TIME LEFT FOR GOALS:

MUST DO

- ☐ ....
- ☐ ....
- ☐ ....

IF TIME

- ☐ ....
- ☐ ....
- ☐ ....

CREATIVE PLAY

....
....
....
....
....
....

DAILY PLANNER

RELATIONSHIPS NURTURED
....
....
....
....
....
....

TODAY'S POSITIVES
....
....
....
....
....
....

Notes

DAILY CHALLENGE
Send a thank-you note to someone who has positively impacted your journey as an artist.

DAILY PLANNER

TODAY'S DATE:

TODAY'S FOCUS:

Today's Events

- 12:00
- 1:00
- 2:00
- 3:00
- 4:00
- 5:00
- 6:00
- 7:00
- 8:00
- 9:00
- 10:00
- 11:00
- 12:00
- 1:00
- 2:00
- 3:00
- 4:00
- 5:00
- 6:00
- 7:00
- 8:00
- 9:00
- 10:00
- 11:00
- 12:00

CURRENT FOCUS GOALS

TIME LEFT FOR GOALS:

MUST DO

- [ ]
- [ ]
- [ ]

IF TIME

- [ ]
- [ ]
- [ ]

CREATIVE PLAY

RELATIONSHIPS NURTURED

....
....
....
....
....
....

TODAY'S POSITIVES

....
....
....
....
....
....

Notes

DAILY CHALLENGE
Organize and archive your old audition footage.

DAILY PLANNER

TODAY'S DATE:	TODAY'S FOCUS:

Today's Events

12:00
1:00
2:00
3:00
4:00
5:00
6:00
7:00
8:00
9:00
10:00
11:00
12:00
1:00
2:00
3:00
4:00
5:00
6:00
7:00
8:00
9:00
10:00
11:00
12:00

CURRENT FOCUS GOALS

....
....
....
....
....
....

TIME LEFT FOR GOALS:

MUST DO
☐ ....
☐ ....
☐ ....

IF TIME
☐ ....
☐ ....
☐ ....

CREATIVE PLAY
....
....
....
....
....
....

RELATIONSHIPS NURTURED

....
....
....
....
....
....

TODAY'S POSITIVES

....
....
....
....
....
....

Notes

DAILY CHALLENGE
Step outside your comfort zone—perform something totally different from your usual roles.

TODO'S DATE:

TODAY'S FOCUS:

Today's Events

- 12:00
- 1:00
- 2:00
- 3:00
- 4:00
- 5:00
- 6:00
- 7:00
- 8:00
- 9:00
- 10:00
- 11:00
- 12:00
- 1:00
- 2:00
- 3:00
- 4:00
- 5:00
- 6:00
- 7:00
- 8:00
- 9:00
- 10:00
- 11:00
- 12:00

CURRENT FOCUS GOALS

....
....
....
....
....
....

TIME LEFT FOR GOALS:

MUST DO

☐ ....
☐ ....
☐ ....

IF TIME

☐ ....
☐ ....
☐ ....

CREATIVE PLAY

....
....
....
....
....
....

DAILY PLANNER

RELATIONSHIPS NURTURED
....
....
....
....
....
....

TODAY'S POSITIVES
....
....
....
....
....
....

Notes

DAILY CHALLENGE
Drink an extra glass of water today.

DAILY PLANNER

TODAY'S DATE:	TODAY'S FOCUS:

Today's Events

- 12:00
- 1:00
- 2:00
- 3:00
- 4:00
- 5:00
- 6:00
- 7:00
- 8:00
- 9:00
- 10:00
- 11:00
- 12:00
- 1:00
- 2:00
- 3:00
- 4:00
- 5:00
- 6:00
- 7:00
- 8:00
- 9:00
- 10:00
- 11:00
- 12:00

CURRENT FOCUS GOALS

....
....
....
....
....

TIME LEFT FOR GOALS:

MUST DO

☐ ....
☐ ....
☐ ....

IF TIME

☐ ....
☐ ....
☐ ....

CREATIVE PLAY

....
....
....
....
....
....
....

RELATIONSHIPS NURTURED

....
....
....
....
....
....

TODAY'S POSITIVES

....
....
....
....
....
....

Notes

DAILY CHALLENGE
Watch a new-to-you indie film. Then write a gratitude email to someone on the creative team.

 **DAILY PLANNER**

| TODAY'S DATE: | TODAY'S FOCUS: |

Today's Events

- 12:00
- 1:00
- 2:00
- 3:00
- 4:00
- 5:00
- 6:00
- 7:00
- 8:00
- 9:00
- 10:00
- 11:00
- 12:00
- 1:00
- 2:00
- 3:00
- 4:00
- 5:00
- 6:00
- 7:00
- 8:00
- 9:00
- 10:00
- 11:00
- 12:00

CURRENT FOCUS GOALS

....
....
....
....
....
....

TIME LEFT FOR GOALS:

MUST DO

☐ ....
☐ ....
☐ ....

IF TIME

☐ ....
☐ ....
☐ ....

CREATIVE PLAY

....
....
....
....
....
....
....

RELATIONSHIPS NURTURED

....
....
....
....
....
....

TODAY'S POSITIVES

....
....
....
....
....
....

Notes

DAILY CHALLENGE
Try a digital detox—turn off all your devices for 1 hour.

DAILY PLANNER

TODAY'S DATE:

TODAY'S FOCUS:

Today's Events

- 12:00
- 1:00
- 2:00
- 3:00
- 4:00
- 5:00
- 6:00
- 7:00
- 8:00
- 9:00
- 10:00
- 11:00
- 12:00
- 1:00
- 2:00
- 3:00
- 4:00
- 5:00
- 6:00
- 7:00
- 8:00
- 9:00
- 10:00
- 11:00
- 12:00

CURRENT FOCUS GOALS

TIME LEFT FOR GOALS:

MUST DO
- [ ]
- [ ]
- [ ]

IF TIME
- [ ]
- [ ]
- [ ]

CREATIVE PLAY

DAILY PLANNER

RELATIONSHIPS NURTURED

....
....
....
....
....
....

TODAY'S POSITIVES

....
....
....
....
....
....

Notes

DAILY CHALLENGE
Review your actor bio and make any necessary updates.

DAILY PLANNER

TODAY'S DATE:

TODAY'S FOCUS:

Today's Events

12:00
1:00
2:00
3:00
4:00
5:00
6:00
7:00
8:00
9:00
10:00
11:00
12:00
1:00
2:00
3:00
4:00
5:00
6:00
7:00
8:00
9:00
10:00
11:00
12:00

CURRENT FOCUS GOALS

....
....
....
....
....
....

TIME LEFT FOR GOALS:

MUST DO

☐ ....
☐ ....
☐ ....

IF TIME

☐ ....
☐ ....
☐ ....

CREATIVE PLAY

....
....
....
....
....
....
....

DAILY PLANNER

RELATIONSHIPS NURTURED

....
....
....
....
....
....

TODAY'S POSITIVES

....
....
....
....
....
....

Notes

DAILY CHALLENGE
Write the character breakdown for a role you'd love to play.

DAILY PLANNER

| TODAY'S DATE: | TODAY'S FOCUS: |

Today's Events

- 12:00
- 1:00
- 2:00
- 3:00
- 4:00
- 5:00
- 6:00
- 7:00
- 8:00
- 9:00
- 10:00
- 11:00
- 12:00
- 1:00
- 2:00
- 3:00
- 4:00
- 5:00
- 6:00
- 7:00
- 8:00
- 9:00
- 10:00
- 11:00
- 12:00

CURRENT FOCUS GOALS

....
....
....
....
....
....

TIME LEFT FOR GOALS:

MUST DO

- ☐ ....
- ☐ ....
- ☐ ....

IF TIME

- ☐ ....
- ☐ ....
- ☐ ....

CREATIVE PLAY

....
....
....
....
....
....
....

RELATIONSHIPS NURTURED

....
....
....
....
....
....

TODAY'S POSITIVES

....
....
....
....
....
....

Notes

DAILY CHALLENGE
Review your actor resume and make any necessary updates.

DAILY PLANNER

TODAY'S DATE:

TODAY'S FOCUS:

Today's Events

12:00
1:00
2:00
3:00
4:00
5:00
6:00
7:00
8:00
9:00
10:00
11:00
12:00
1:00
2:00
3:00
4:00
5:00
6:00
7:00
8:00
9:00
10:00
11:00
12:00

CURRENT FOCUS GOALS

....
....
....
....
....
....

TIME LEFT FOR GOALS:

MUST DO

☐ ....
☐ ....
☐ ....

IF TIME

☐ ....
☐ ....
☐ ....

CREATIVE PLAY

....
....
....
....
....
....
....

DAILY PLANNER

RELATIONSHIPS NURTURED

....
....
....
....
....
....

TODAY'S POSITIVES

....
....
....
....
....
....

Notes

DAILY CHALLENGE
Take yourself on an artist date.

DAILY PLANNER

| TODAY'S DATE: | TODAY'S FOCUS: |

Today's Events

12:00
1:00
2:00
3:00
4:00
5:00
6:00
7:00
8:00
9:00
10:00
11:00
12:00
1:00
2:00
3:00
4:00
5:00
6:00
7:00
8:00
9:00
10:00
11:00
12:00

CURRENT FOCUS GOALS

....
....
....
....
....
....

| TIME LEFT FOR GOALS: |

MUST DO

☐ ....
☐ ....
☐ ....

IF TIME

☐ ....
☐ ....
☐ ....

CREATIVE PLAY

....
....
....
....
....
....
....
....

DAILY PLANNER

RELATIONSHIPS NURTURED

....
....
....
....
....
....

TODAY'S POSITIVES

....
....
....
....
....
....

Notes

DAILY CHALLENGE
Spend 10 minutes clearing out your email inbox.

 **DAILY PLANNER**

TODAY'S DATE:

TODAY'S FOCUS:

Today's Events

12:00
1:00
2:00
3:00
4:00
5:00
6:00
7:00
8:00
9:00
10:00
11:00
12:00
1:00
2:00
3:00
4:00
5:00
6:00
7:00
8:00
9:00
10:00
11:00
12:00

CURRENT FOCUS GOALS

....
....
....
....
....
....

TIME LEFT FOR GOALS:

MUST DO

☐ ....
☐ ....
☐ ....

IF TIME

☐ ....
☐ ....
☐ ....

CREATIVE PLAY

....
....
....
....
....
....

RELATIONSHIPS NURTURED

....
....
....
....
....
....

TODAY'S POSITIVES

....
....
....
....
....
....

Notes

DAILY CHALLENGE
Rehearse a monologue in five different emotional tones.

| TODAY'S DATE: | TODAY'S FOCUS: |

Today's Events

- 12:00
- 1:00
- 2:00
- 3:00
- 4:00
- 5:00
- 6:00
- 7:00
- 8:00
- 9:00
- 10:00
- 11:00
- 12:00
- 1:00
- 2:00
- 3:00
- 4:00
- 5:00
- 6:00
- 7:00
- 8:00
- 9:00
- 10:00
- 11:00
- 12:00

CURRENT FOCUS GOALS

....
....
....
....
....
....

| TIME LEFT FOR GOALS: |

MUST DO

☐ ....
☐ ....
☐ ....

IF TIME

☐ ....
☐ ....
☐ ....

CREATIVE PLAY

....
....
....
....
....
....
....

RELATIONSHIPS NURTURED

....
....
....
....
....
....

TODAY'S POSITIVES

....
....
....
....
....
....

Notes

DAILY CHALLENGE
Listen to an interview with your favorite director or actor to learn about their creative process.

DAILY PLANNER

TODAY'S DATE:

TODAY'S FOCUS:

Today's Events

12:00
1:00
2:00
3:00
4:00
5:00
6:00
7:00
8:00
9:00
10:00
11:00
12:00
1:00
2:00
3:00
4:00
5:00
6:00
7:00
8:00
9:00
10:00
11:00
12:00

CURRENT FOCUS GOALS

....
....
....
....
....
....

TIME LEFT FOR GOALS:

MUST DO

☐ ....
☐ ....
☐ ....

IF TIME

☐ ....
☐ ....
☐ ....

CREATIVE PLAY

....
....
....
....
....
....
....

RELATIONSHIPS NURTURED
....
....
....
....
....

TODAY'S POSITIVES
....
....
....
....
....

Notes

DAILY CHALLENGE
Acting like a proud parent, rewatch old acting footage of yourself.

DAILY PLANNER

TODAY'S DATE:	TODAY'S FOCUS:

Today's Events

- 12:00
- 1:00
- 2:00
- 3:00
- 4:00
- 5:00
- 6:00
- 7:00
- 8:00
- 9:00
- 10:00
- 11:00
- 12:00
- 1:00
- 2:00
- 3:00
- 4:00
- 5:00
- 6:00
- 7:00
- 8:00
- 9:00
- 10:00
- 11:00
- 12:00

CURRENT FOCUS GOALS

....
....
....
....
....
....

TIME LEFT FOR GOALS:

MUST DO

- ☐ ....
- ☐ ....
- ☐ ....

IF TIME

- ☐ ....
- ☐ ....
- ☐ ....

CREATIVE PLAY

....
....
....
....
....
....

RELATIONSHIPS NURTURED

....
....
....
....
....
....

TODAY'S POSITIVES

....
....
....
....
....
....

Notes

DAILY CHALLENGE
Write a letter of encouragement to your 6-year-old self.

DAILY PLANNER

TODAY'S DATE:

TODAY'S FOCUS:

Today's Events

- 12:00
- 1:00
- 2:00
- 3:00
- 4:00
- 5:00
- 6:00
- 7:00
- 8:00
- 9:00
- 10:00
- 11:00
- 12:00
- 1:00
- 2:00
- 3:00
- 4:00
- 5:00
- 6:00
- 7:00
- 8:00
- 9:00
- 10:00
- 11:00
- 12:00

CURRENT FOCUS GOALS

....
....
....
....
....
....

TIME LEFT FOR GOALS:

MUST DO

☐ ....
☐ ....
☐ ....

IF TIME

☐ ....
☐ ....
☐ ....

CREATIVE PLAY

....
....
....
....
....
....

DAILY PLANNER

RELATIONSHIPS NURTURED
....
....
....
....
....

TODAY'S POSITIVES
....
....
....
....
....

Notes

DAILY CHALLENGE
Find a local film festival. Make plans to attend.

DAILY PLANNER

| TODAY'S DATE: | TODAY'S FOCUS: |

Today's Events

- 12:00
- 1:00
- 2:00
- 3:00
- 4:00
- 5:00
- 6:00
- 7:00
- 8:00
- 9:00
- 10:00
- 11:00
- 12:00
- 1:00
- 2:00
- 3:00
- 4:00
- 5:00
- 6:00
- 7:00
- 8:00
- 9:00
- 10:00
- 11:00
- 12:00

CURRENT FOCUS GOALS

....
....
....
....
....
....

TIME LEFT FOR GOALS:

MUST DO

☐ ....
☐ ....
☐ ....

IF TIME

☐ ....
☐ ....
☐ ....

CREATIVE PLAY

....
....
....
....
....
....

RELATIONSHIPS NURTURED

....
....
....
....
....
....

TODAY'S POSITIVES

....
....
....
....
....
....

Notes

DAILY CHALLENGE
Record a quick behind-the-scenes video of your preparation process for social media.

DAILY PLANNER

TODAY'S DATE:

TODAY'S FOCUS:

Today's Events

12:00
1:00
2:00
3:00
4:00
5:00
6:00
7:00
8:00
9:00
10:00
11:00
12:00
1:00
2:00
3:00
4:00
5:00
6:00
7:00
8:00
9:00
10:00
11:00
12:00

CURRENT FOCUS GOALS

....
....
....
....
....
....

TIME LEFT FOR GOALS:

MUST DO

☐ ....
☐ ....
☐ ....

IF TIME

☐ ....
☐ ....
☐ ....

CREATIVE PLAY

....
....
....
....
....
....
....

RELATIONSHIPS NURTURED

....
....
....
....
....
....

TODAY'S POSITIVES

....
....
....
....
....
....

Notes

DAILY CHALLENGE
Try a 15-minute guided meditation.

DAILY PLANNER

TODAY'S DATE:	TODAY'S FOCUS:

Today's Events

- 12:00
- 1:00
- 2:00
- 3:00
- 4:00
- 5:00
- 6:00
- 7:00
- 8:00
- 9:00
- 10:00
- 11:00
- 12:00
- 1:00
- 2:00
- 3:00
- 4:00
- 5:00
- 6:00
- 7:00
- 8:00
- 9:00
- 10:00
- 11:00
- 12:00

CURRENT FOCUS GOALS

....
....
....
....
....
....

TIME LEFT FOR GOALS:

MUST DO

- [ ] ....
- [ ] ....
- [ ] ....

IF TIME

- [ ] ....
- [ ] ....
- [ ] ....

CREATIVE PLAY

....
....
....
....
....
....
....
....

RELATIONSHIPS NURTURED

....
....
....
....
....
....

TODAY'S POSITIVES

....
....
....
....
....
....

Notes

DAILY CHALLENGE
Identify one unnecessary expense you can cut this month.

 **DAILY PLANNER**

| TODAY'S DATE: | TODAY'S FOCUS: |

Today's Events

12:00
1:00
2:00
3:00
4:00
5:00
6:00
7:00
8:00
9:00
10:00
11:00
12:00
1:00
2:00
3:00
4:00
5:00
6:00
7:00
8:00
9:00
10:00
11:00
12:00

CURRENT FOCUS GOALS

....
....
....
....
....
....

| TIME LEFT FOR GOALS: |

MUST DO

☐ ....
☐ ....
☐ ....

IF TIME

☐ ....
☐ ....
☐ ....

CREATIVE PLAY

....
....
....
....
....
....
....

RELATIONSHIPS NURTURED

....
....
....
....
....
....

TODAY'S POSITIVES

....
....
....
....
....
....

Notes

DAILY CHALLENGE
Self-submit to at least 1 breakdown today.

DAILY PLANNER

| TODAY'S DATE: | TODAY'S FOCUS: |

Today's Events

- 12:00
- 1:00
- 2:00
- 3:00
- 4:00
- 5:00
- 6:00
- 7:00
- 8:00
- 9:00
- 10:00
- 11:00
- 12:00
- 1:00
- 2:00
- 3:00
- 4:00
- 5:00
- 6:00
- 7:00
- 8:00
- 9:00
- 10:00
- 11:00
- 12:00

CURRENT FOCUS GOALS

....
....
....
....
....
....

| TIME LEFT FOR GOALS: |

MUST DO

☐ ....
☐ ....
☐ ....

IF TIME

☐ ....
☐ ....
☐ ....

CREATIVE PLAY

....
....
....
....
....
....
....

RELATIONSHIPS NURTURED

....
....
....
....
....
....

TODAY'S POSITIVES

....
....
....
....
....
....

Notes

DAILY CHALLENGE
Try a new acting exercise you've never done before.

DAILY PLANNER

| TODAY'S DATE: | TODAY'S FOCUS: |

Today's Events

12:00
1:00
2:00
3:00
4:00
5:00
6:00
7:00
8:00
9:00
10:00
11:00
12:00
1:00
2:00
3:00
4:00
5:00
6:00
7:00
8:00
9:00
10:00
11:00
12:00

CURRENT FOCUS GOALS

....
....
....
....
....
....

| TIME LEFT FOR GOALS: |

MUST DO

☐ ....
☐ ....
☐ ....

IF TIME

☐ ....
☐ ....
☐ ....

CREATIVE PLAY

....
....
....
....
....
....

DAILY PLANNER

RELATIONSHIPS NURTURED

....
....
....
....
....
....

TODAY'S POSITIVES

....
....
....
....
....
....

Notes

DAILY CHALLENGE
Start an actor newsletter.

DAILY PLANNER

| TODAY'S DATE: | TODAY'S FOCUS: |

Today's Events

12:00
1:00
2:00
3:00
4:00
5:00
6:00
7:00
8:00
9:00
10:00
11:00
12:00
1:00
2:00
3:00
4:00
5:00
6:00
7:00
8:00
9:00
10:00
11:00
12:00

CURRENT FOCUS GOALS

....
....
....
....
....
....

| TIME LEFT FOR GOALS: |

MUST DO

☐ ....
☐ ....
☐ ....

IF TIME

☐ ....
☐ ....
☐ ....

CREATIVE PLAY

....
....
....
....
....
....
....

RELATIONSHIPS NURTURED

....
....
....
....
....
....

TODAY'S POSITIVES

....
....
....
....
....
....

Notes

DAILY CHALLENGE
Review your primary headshot. Does this person reflect the types of roles you're currently calling in?

DAILY PLANNER

| TODAY'S DATE: | TODAY'S FOCUS: |

Today's Events

- 12:00
- 1:00
- 2:00
- 3:00
- 4:00
- 5:00
- 6:00
- 7:00
- 8:00
- 9:00
- 10:00
- 11:00
- 12:00
- 1:00
- 2:00
- 3:00
- 4:00
- 5:00
- 6:00
- 7:00
- 8:00
- 9:00
- 10:00
- 11:00
- 12:00

CURRENT FOCUS GOALS

....
....
....
....
....
....

| TIME LEFT FOR GOALS: |

MUST DO

- ☐ ....
- ☐ ....
- ☐ ....

IF TIME

- ☐ ....
- ☐ ....
- ☐ ....

CREATIVE PLAY

....
....
....
....
....
....

RELATIONSHIPS NURTURED

....
....
....
....
....
....

TODAY'S POSITIVES

....
....
....
....
....
....

Notes

DAILY CHALLENGE
Spend 10 minutes doing deep, intentional breathing exercises to improve vocal control.

 **DAILY PLANNER**

TODAY'S DATE:	TODAY'S FOCUS:

Today's Events

CURRENT FOCUS GOALS

12:00
1:00
2:00
3:00
4:00
5:00
6:00
7:00
8:00
9:00
10:00
11:00
12:00
1:00
2:00
3:00
4:00
5:00
6:00
7:00
8:00
9:00
10:00
11:00
12:00

TIME LEFT FOR GOALS:

MUST DO

☐ ....
☐ ....
☐ ....

IF TIME

☐ ....
☐ ....
☐ ....

CREATIVE PLAY

RELATIONSHIPS NURTURED

....
....
....
....
....
....

TODAY'S POSITIVES

....
....
....
....
....
....

Notes

DAILY CHALLENGE
Reread a children's book you loved growing up.

DAILY PLANNER

TODAY'S DATE:

TODAY'S FOCUS:

Today's Events

12:00
1:00
2:00
3:00
4:00
5:00
6:00
7:00
8:00
9:00
10:00
11:00
12:00
1:00
2:00
3:00
4:00
5:00
6:00
7:00
8:00
9:00
10:00
11:00
12:00

CURRENT FOCUS GOALS

....
....
....
....
....
....

TIME LEFT FOR GOALS:

MUST DO

☐ ....
☐ ....
☐ ....

IF TIME

☐ ....
☐ ....
☐ ....

CREATIVE PLAY

....
....
....
....
....
....

RELATIONSHIPS NURTURED

....
....
....
....
....
....

TODAY'S POSITIVES

....
....
....
....
....
....

Notes

DAILY CHALLENGE
Review your demo reel or acting clips. Do they showcase the quality of work you can produce today?

DAILY PLANNER

110

TODAY'S DATE:

TODAY'S FOCUS:

Today's Events

12:00
1:00
2:00
3:00
4:00
5:00
6:00
7:00
8:00
9:00
10:00
11:00
12:00
1:00
2:00
3:00
4:00
5:00
6:00
7:00
8:00
9:00
10:00
11:00
12:00

CURRENT FOCUS GOALS

....
....
....
....
....
....

TIME LEFT FOR GOALS:

MUST DO

☐ ....
☐ ....
☐ ....

IF TIME

☐ ....
☐ ....
☐ ....

CREATIVE PLAY

....
....
....
....
....
....

DAILY PLANNER

RELATIONSHIPS NURTURED

....
....
....
....
....

TODAY'S POSITIVES

....
....
....
....
....

Notes

DAILY CHALLENGE
Craft your artist's mission statement.

 **DAILY PLANNER**

| TODAY'S DATE: | TODAY'S FOCUS: |

Today's Events

- 12:00
- 1:00
- 2:00
- 3:00
- 4:00
- 5:00
- 6:00
- 7:00
- 8:00
- 9:00
- 10:00
- 11:00
- 12:00
- 1:00
- 2:00
- 3:00
- 4:00
- 5:00
- 6:00
- 7:00
- 8:00
- 9:00
- 10:00
- 11:00
- 12:00

CURRENT FOCUS GOALS

....
....
....
....
....
....

| TIME LEFT FOR GOALS: |

MUST DO

☐ ....
☐ ....
☐ ....

IF TIME

☐ ....
☐ ....
☐ ....

CREATIVE PLAY

....
....
....
....
....
....

RELATIONSHIPS NURTURED

....
....
....
....
....
....

TODAY'S POSITIVES

....
....
....
....
....
....

Notes

DAILY CHALLENGE
Review your self-tape setup. Can you set it up and break it down in under 2 minutes?

DAILY PLANNER

TODAY'S DATE:

TODAY'S FOCUS:

Today's Events

12:00
1:00
2:00
3:00
4:00
5:00
6:00
7:00
8:00
9:00
10:00
11:00
12:00
1:00
2:00
3:00
4:00
5:00
6:00
7:00
8:00
9:00
10:00
11:00
12:00

CURRENT FOCUS GOALS

TIME LEFT FOR GOALS:

MUST DO

☐
☐
☐

IF TIME

☐
☐
☐

CREATIVE PLAY

RELATIONSHIPS NURTURED

....
....
....
....
....
....

TODAY'S POSITIVES

....
....
....
....
....
....

Notes

DAILY CHALLENGE
Brainstorm 10 alternative lives to the one you're living now. Who would you be?

DAILY PLANNER

TODAY'S DATE:

TODAY'S FOCUS:

Today's Events

12:00
1:00
2:00
3:00
4:00
5:00
6:00
7:00
8:00
9:00
10:00
11:00
12:00
1:00
2:00
3:00
4:00
5:00
6:00
7:00
8:00
9:00
10:00
11:00
12:00

CURRENT FOCUS GOALS

....
....
....
....
....
....
....

TIME LEFT FOR GOALS:

MUST DO

☐ ....
☐ ....
☐ ....

IF TIME

☐ ....
☐ ....
☐ ....

CREATIVE PLAY

....
....
....
....
....
....
....

RELATIONSHIPS NURTURED

....
....
....
....
....
....

TODAY'S POSITIVES

....
....
....
....
....
....

Notes

DAILY CHALLENGE
Delete any apps you haven't used in the last month.

DAILY PLANNER

| TODAY'S DATE: | TODAY'S FOCUS: |

Today's Events

12:00
1:00
2:00
3:00
4:00
5:00
6:00
7:00
8:00
9:00
10:00
11:00
12:00
1:00
2:00
3:00
4:00
5:00
6:00
7:00
8:00
9:00
10:00
11:00
12:00

CURRENT FOCUS GOALS

....
....
....
....
....
....

| TIME LEFT FOR GOALS: |

MUST DO

☐ ....
☐ ....
☐ ....

IF TIME

☐ ....
☐ ....
☐ ....

CREATIVE PLAY

....
....
....
....
....
....

RELATIONSHIPS NURTURED

....

....

....

....

....

....

TODAY'S POSITIVES

....

....

....

....

....

....

Notes

DAILY CHALLENGE
Order your favorite meal, just because.

 **DAILY PLANNER**

TODAY'S DATE:

TODAY'S FOCUS:

Today's Events

- 12:00
- 1:00
- 2:00
- 3:00
- 4:00
- 5:00
- 6:00
- 7:00
- 8:00
- 9:00
- 10:00
- 11:00
- 12:00
- 1:00
- 2:00
- 3:00
- 4:00
- 5:00
- 6:00
- 7:00
- 8:00
- 9:00
- 10:00
- 11:00
- 12:00

CURRENT FOCUS GOALS

TIME LEFT FOR GOALS:

MUST DO
- ☐
- ☐
- ☐

IF TIME
- ☐
- ☐
- ☐

CREATIVE PLAY

DAILY PLANNER

RELATIONSHIPS NURTURED

....
....
....
....
....
....

TODAY'S POSITIVES

....
....
....
....
....
....

Notes

DAILY CHALLENGE
Read the screenplay to your favorite film.

DAILY PLANNER

TODAY'S DATE:	TODAY'S FOCUS:

Today's Events

- 12:00
- 1:00
- 2:00
- 3:00
- 4:00
- 5:00
- 6:00
- 7:00
- 8:00
- 9:00
- 10:00
- 11:00
- 12:00
- 1:00
- 2:00
- 3:00
- 4:00
- 5:00
- 6:00
- 7:00
- 8:00
- 9:00
- 10:00
- 11:00
- 12:00

CURRENT FOCUS GOALS

....
....
....
....
....
....

TIME LEFT FOR GOALS:

MUST DO

- ☐ ....
- ☐ ....
- ☐ ....

IF TIME

- ☐ ....
- ☐ ....
- ☐ ....

CREATIVE PLAY

....
....
....
....
....
....
....

DAILY PLANNER

RELATIONSHIPS NURTURED

....
....
....
....
....
....

TODAY'S POSITIVES

....
....
....
....
....
....

Notes

DAILY CHALLENGE
Share an acting win on your favorite social media platform.

 **DAILY PLANNER**

| TODAY'S DATE: | TODAY'S FOCUS: |

Today's Events

12:00
1:00
2:00
3:00
4:00
5:00
6:00
7:00
8:00
9:00
10:00
11:00
12:00
1:00
2:00
3:00
4:00
5:00
6:00
7:00
8:00
9:00
10:00
11:00
12:00

CURRENT FOCUS GOALS

....
....
....
....
....
....

TIME LEFT FOR GOALS:

MUST DO

☐ ....
☐ ....
☐ ....

IF TIME

☐ ....
☐ ....
☐ ....

CREATIVE PLAY

....
....
....
....
....
....

RELATIONSHIPS NURTURED

....
....
....
....
....
....

TODAY'S POSITIVES

....
....
....
....
....
....

Notes

DAILY CHALLENGE
Research artist grants or scholarships you can apply for.

DAILY PLANNER

| TODAY'S DATE: | TODAY'S FOCUS: |

Today's Events

12:00
1:00
2:00
3:00
4:00
5:00
6:00
7:00
8:00
9:00
10:00
11:00
12:00
1:00
2:00
3:00
4:00
5:00
6:00
7:00
8:00
9:00
10:00
11:00
12:00

CURRENT FOCUS GOALS

....
....
....
....
....
....

| TIME LEFT FOR GOALS: |

MUST DO

☐ ....
☐ ....
☐ ....

IF TIME

☐ ....
☐ ....
☐ ....

CREATIVE PLAY

....
....
....
....
....
....
....

RELATIONSHIPS NURTURED

....
....
....
....
....
....

TODAY'S POSITIVES

....
....
....
....
....
....

Notes

DAILY CHALLENGE
Find a quiet outdoor space to sit for 10 minutes to recharge.

 **DAILY PLANNER**

| TODAY'S DATE: | TODAY'S FOCUS: |

Today's Events

- 12:00
- 1:00
- 2:00
- 3:00
- 4:00
- 5:00
- 6:00
- 7:00
- 8:00
- 9:00
- 10:00
- 11:00
- 12:00
- 1:00
- 2:00
- 3:00
- 4:00
- 5:00
- 6:00
- 7:00
- 8:00
- 9:00
- 10:00
- 11:00
- 12:00

CURRENT FOCUS GOALS

....
....
....
....
....

| TIME LEFT FOR GOALS: |

MUST DO

☐ ....
☐ ....
☐ ....

IF TIME

☐ ....
☐ ....
☐ ....

CREATIVE PLAY

....
....
....
....
....
....

DAILY PLANNER

RELATIONSHIPS NURTURED

....
....
....
....
....
....

TODAY'S POSITIVES

....
....
....
....
....
....

Notes

DAILY CHALLENGE
Unsubscribe from 3 newsletters you don't read.

DAILY PLANNER

TODAY'S DATE:

TODAY'S FOCUS:

Today's Events

12:00
1:00
2:00
3:00
4:00
5:00
6:00
7:00
8:00
9:00
10:00
11:00
12:00
1:00
2:00
3:00
4:00
5:00
6:00
7:00
8:00
9:00
10:00
11:00
12:00

CURRENT FOCUS GOALS

TIME LEFT FOR GOALS:

MUST DO
☐
☐
☐

IF TIME
☐
☐
☐

CREATIVE PLAY

DAILY PLANNER

RELATIONSHIPS NURTURED
....
....
....
....
....
....

TODAY'S POSITIVES
....
....
....
....
....
....

Notes

DAILY CHALLENGE
Go for a 20-minute, device-free walk.

 **DAILY PLANNER**

TODAY'S DATE:

TODAY'S FOCUS:

Today's Events

12:00
1:00
2:00
3:00
4:00
5:00
6:00
7:00
8:00
9:00
10:00
11:00
12:00
1:00
2:00
3:00
4:00
5:00
6:00
7:00
8:00
9:00
10:00
11:00
12:00

CURRENT FOCUS GOALS

TIME LEFT FOR GOALS:

MUST DO
☐ ....
☐ ....
☐ ....

IF TIME
☐ ....
☐ ....
☐ ....

CREATIVE PLAY

DAILY PLANNER

RELATIONSHIPS NURTURED

....
....
....
....
....

TODAY'S POSITIVES

....
....
....
....
....

Notes

DAILY CHALLENGE
Watch a TED Talk about creativity.

DAILY PLANNER

TODAY'S DATE:

TODAY'S FOCUS:

Today's Events

- 12:00
- 1:00
- 2:00
- 3:00
- 4:00
- 5:00
- 6:00
- 7:00
- 8:00
- 9:00
- 10:00
- 11:00
- 12:00
- 1:00
- 2:00
- 3:00
- 4:00
- 5:00
- 6:00
- 7:00
- 8:00
- 9:00
- 10:00
- 11:00
- 12:00

CURRENT FOCUS GOALS

TIME LEFT FOR GOALS:

MUST DO
- ☐
- ☐
- ☐

IF TIME
- ☐
- ☐
- ☐

CREATIVE PLAY

RELATIONSHIPS NURTURED

....
....
....
....
....
....

TODAY'S POSITIVES

....
....
....
....
....
....

Notes

DAILY CHALLENGE
Reconnect with a peer whose work you respect.

| TODAY'S DATE: | TODAY'S FOCUS: |

Today's Events

CURRENT FOCUS GOALS

12:00
1:00
2:00
3:00
4:00
5:00
6:00
7:00

TIME LEFT FOR GOALS:

8:00
9:00
10:00
11:00

MUST DO

☐ ....
☐ ....
☐ ....

12:00
1:00

IF TIME

☐ ....
☐ ....
☐ ....

2:00
3:00
4:00

CREATIVE PLAY

5:00
6:00
7:00
8:00
9:00
10:00
11:00
12:00

DAILY PLANNER

RELATIONSHIPS NURTURED
....
....
....
....
....
....

TODAY'S POSITIVES
....
....
....
....
....
....

Notes

DAILY CHALLENGE
Wear your favorite article of clothing, just because.

DAILY PLANNER

TODAY'S DATE:

TODAY'S FOCUS:

Today's Events

- 12:00
- 1:00
- 2:00
- 3:00
- 4:00
- 5:00
- 6:00
- 7:00
- 8:00
- 9:00
- 10:00
- 11:00
- 12:00
- 1:00
- 2:00
- 3:00
- 4:00
- 5:00
- 6:00
- 7:00
- 8:00
- 9:00
- 10:00
- 11:00
- 12:00

CURRENT FOCUS GOALS

TIME LEFT FOR GOALS:

MUST DO

- [ ]
- [ ]
- [ ]

IF TIME

- [ ]
- [ ]
- [ ]

CREATIVE PLAY

RELATIONSHIPS NURTURED

....
....
....
....
....
....

TODAY'S POSITIVES

....
....
....
....
....
....

Notes

DAILY CHALLENGE
Watch a performance from an actor you admire and take notes on what stands out.

DAILY PLANNER

TODAY'S DATE:	TODAY'S FOCUS:

Today's Events

CURRENT FOCUS GOALS

12:00
1:00
2:00
3:00
4:00
5:00
6:00
7:00

TIME LEFT FOR GOALS:

8:00
9:00
10:00
11:00

MUST DO

☐ ....
☐ ....
☐ ....

12:00
1:00
2:00
3:00
4:00

IF TIME

☐ ....
☐ ....
☐ ....

5:00
6:00
7:00
8:00
9:00
10:00
11:00
12:00

CREATIVE PLAY

RELATIONSHIPS NURTURED

....
....
....
....
....
....

TODAY'S POSITIVES

....
....
....
....
....
....

Notes

DAILY CHALLENGE
Share an interesting industry article with someone else.

DAILY PLANNER

TODAY'S DATE:	TODAY'S FOCUS:

Today's Events

- 12:00
- 1:00
- 2:00
- 3:00
- 4:00
- 5:00
- 6:00
- 7:00
- 8:00
- 9:00
- 10:00
- 11:00
- 12:00
- 1:00
- 2:00
- 3:00
- 4:00
- 5:00
- 6:00
- 7:00
- 8:00
- 9:00
- 10:00
- 11:00
- 12:00

CURRENT FOCUS GOALS

....
....
....
....
....

TIME LEFT FOR GOALS:

MUST DO

- ☐ ....
- ☐ ....
- ☐ ....

IF TIME

- ☐ ....
- ☐ ....
- ☐ ....

CREATIVE PLAY

....
....
....
....
....
....

RELATIONSHIPS NURTURED

....
....
....
....
....
....

TODAY'S POSITIVES

....
....
....
....
....
....

Notes

DAILY CHALLENGE
Create a separate bank account for your acting-related income and expenses.

DAILY PLANNER

| TODAY'S DATE: | TODAY'S FOCUS: |

Today's Events

12:00
1:00
2:00
3:00
4:00
5:00
6:00
7:00
8:00
9:00
10:00
11:00
12:00
1:00
2:00
3:00
4:00
5:00
6:00
7:00
8:00
9:00
10:00
11:00
12:00

CURRENT FOCUS GOALS

....
....
....
....
....
....

| TIME LEFT FOR GOALS: |

MUST DO

☐ ....
☐ ....
☐ ....

IF TIME

☐ ....
☐ ....
☐ ....

CREATIVE PLAY

....
....
....
....
....
....

DAILY PLANNER

RELATIONSHIPS NURTURED

....
....
....
....
....
....

TODAY'S POSITIVES

....
....
....
....
....
....

Notes

DAILY CHALLENGE
Re-read your favorite play.

DAILY PLANNER

| TODAY'S DATE: | TODAY'S FOCUS: |

Today's Events

- 12:00
- 1:00
- 2:00
- 3:00
- 4:00
- 5:00
- 6:00
- 7:00
- 8:00
- 9:00
- 10:00
- 11:00
- 12:00
- 1:00
- 2:00
- 3:00
- 4:00
- 5:00
- 6:00
- 7:00
- 8:00
- 9:00
- 10:00
- 11:00
- 12:00

CURRENT FOCUS GOALS

....
....
....
....
....
....

TIME LEFT FOR GOALS:

MUST DO

☐ ....
☐ ....
☐ ....

IF TIME

☐ ....
☐ ....
☐ ....

CREATIVE PLAY

....
....
....
....
....
....

DAILY PLANNER

RELATIONSHIPS NURTURED
....
....
....
....
....
....

TODAY'S POSITIVES
....
....
....
....
....
....

Notes

DAILY CHALLENGE
Try a new restorative face mask.

DAILY PLANNER

| TODAY'S DATE: | TODAY'S FOCUS: |

Today's Events

- 12:00
- 1:00
- 2:00
- 3:00
- 4:00
- 5:00
- 6:00
- 7:00
- 8:00
- 9:00
- 10:00
- 11:00
- 12:00
- 1:00
- 2:00
- 3:00
- 4:00
- 5:00
- 6:00
- 7:00
- 8:00
- 9:00
- 10:00
- 11:00
- 12:00

CURRENT FOCUS GOALS

....
....
....
....
....

TIME LEFT FOR GOALS:

MUST DO

☐ ....
☐ ....
☐ ....

IF TIME

☐ ....
☐ ....
☐ ....

CREATIVE PLAY

....
....
....
....
....
....
....

DAILY PLANNER

149

RELATIONSHIPS NURTURED

....
....
....
....
....
....

TODAY'S POSITIVES

....
....
....
....
....
....

Notes

DAILY CHALLENGE
Reach out to 3 people and request testimonials for your acting work.

DAILY PLANNER

TODAY'S DATE:

TODAY'S FOCUS:

Today's Events

- 12:00
- 1:00
- 2:00
- 3:00
- 4:00
- 5:00
- 6:00
- 7:00
- 8:00
- 9:00
- 10:00
- 11:00
- 12:00
- 1:00
- 2:00
- 3:00
- 4:00
- 5:00
- 6:00
- 7:00
- 8:00
- 9:00
- 10:00
- 11:00
- 12:00

CURRENT FOCUS GOALS

TIME LEFT FOR GOALS:

MUST DO
- ☐ ...
- ☐ ...
- ☐ ...

IF TIME
- ☐ ...
- ☐ ...
- ☐ ...

CREATIVE PLAY

DAILY PLANNER

RELATIONSHIPS NURTURED
....
....
....
....
....
....

TODAY'S POSITIVES
....
....
....
....
....
....

Notes

DAILY CHALLENGE
Revisit an old monologue you haven't run in a while.

TODAY'S DATE:

TODAY'S FOCUS:

Today's Events

- 12:00
- 1:00
- 2:00
- 3:00
- 4:00
- 5:00
- 6:00
- 7:00
- 8:00
- 9:00
- 10:00
- 11:00
- 12:00
- 1:00
- 2:00
- 3:00
- 4:00
- 5:00
- 6:00
- 7:00
- 8:00
- 9:00
- 10:00
- 11:00
- 12:00

CURRENT FOCUS GOALS

TIME LEFT FOR GOALS:

MUST DO

- ☐
- ☐
- ☐

IF TIME

- ☐
- ☐
- ☐

CREATIVE PLAY

RELATIONSHIPS NURTURED

....
....
....
....
....
....

TODAY'S POSITIVES

....
....
....
....
....
....

Notes

DAILY CHALLENGE
Invite a mentor to lunch.

DAILY PLANNER

TODAY'S DATE:

TODAY'S FOCUS:

Today's Events

- 12:00
- 1:00
- 2:00
- 3:00
- 4:00
- 5:00
- 6:00
- 7:00
- 8:00
- 9:00
- 10:00
- 11:00
- 12:00
- 1:00
- 2:00
- 3:00
- 4:00
- 5:00
- 6:00
- 7:00
- 8:00
- 9:00
- 10:00
- 11:00
- 12:00

CURRENT FOCUS GOALS

TIME LEFT FOR GOALS:

MUST DO
- ☐
- ☐
- ☐

IF TIME
- ☐
- ☐
- ☐

CREATIVE PLAY

RELATIONSHIPS NURTURED

....
....
....
....
....
....

TODAY'S POSITIVES

....
....
....
....
....
....

Notes

DAILY CHALLENGE
Research different ways you can create multiple income streams.

DAILY PLANNER

| TODAY'S DATE: | TODAY'S FOCUS: |

Today's Events

- 12:00
- 1:00
- 2:00
- 3:00
- 4:00
- 5:00
- 6:00
- 7:00
- 8:00
- 9:00
- 10:00
- 11:00
- 12:00
- 1:00
- 2:00
- 3:00
- 4:00
- 5:00
- 6:00
- 7:00
- 8:00
- 9:00
- 10:00
- 11:00
- 12:00

CURRENT FOCUS GOALS

....
....
....
....
....
....

TIME LEFT FOR GOALS:

MUST DO

☐ ....
☐ ....
☐ ....

IF TIME

☐ ....
☐ ....
☐ ....

CREATIVE PLAY

....
....
....
....
....
....

DAILY PLANNER

RELATIONSHIPS NURTURED

....
....
....
....
....
....

TODAY'S POSITIVES

....
....
....
....
....
....

Notes

DAILY CHALLENGE
Set Google Alerts for your name so you're kept in the know.

DAILY PLANNER

TODAY'S DATE:

TODAY'S FOCUS:

Today's Events

- 12:00
- 1:00
- 2:00
- 3:00
- 4:00
- 5:00
- 6:00
- 7:00
- 8:00
- 9:00
- 10:00
- 11:00
- 12:00
- 1:00
- 2:00
- 3:00
- 4:00
- 5:00
- 6:00
- 7:00
- 8:00
- 9:00
- 10:00
- 11:00
- 12:00

CURRENT FOCUS GOALS

TIME LEFT FOR GOALS:

MUST DO
- ☐
- ☐
- ☐

IF TIME
- ☐
- ☐
- ☐

CREATIVE PLAY

RELATIONSHIPS NURTURED

....
....
....
....
....
....

TODAY'S POSITIVES

....
....
....
....
....
....

Notes

DAILY CHALLENGE
Go people-watching and take notes on interesting behaviors or mannerisms.

DAILY PLANNER

TODAY'S DATE:	TODAY'S FOCUS:

Today's Events

- 12:00
- 1:00
- 2:00
- 3:00
- 4:00
- 5:00
- 6:00
- 7:00
- 8:00
- 9:00
- 10:00
- 11:00
- 12:00
- 1:00
- 2:00
- 3:00
- 4:00
- 5:00
- 6:00
- 7:00
- 8:00
- 9:00
- 10:00
- 11:00
- 12:00

CURRENT FOCUS GOALS

....
....
....
....
....
....

TIME LEFT FOR GOALS:

MUST DO

☐ ....
☐ ....
☐ ....

IF TIME

☐ ....
☐ ....
☐ ....

CREATIVE PLAY

....
....
....
....
....
....

DAILY PLANNER

RELATIONSHIPS NURTURED
....
....
....
....
....
....

TODAY'S POSITIVES
....
....
....
....
....
....

Notes

DAILY CHALLENGE
Do a 5-minute "stream of consciousness" free write.

DAILY PLANNER

| TODAY'S DATE: | TODAY'S FOCUS: |

Today's Events

- 12:00
- 1:00
- 2:00
- 3:00
- 4:00
- 5:00
- 6:00
- 7:00
- 8:00
- 9:00
- 10:00
- 11:00
- 12:00
- 1:00
- 2:00
- 3:00
- 4:00
- 5:00
- 6:00
- 7:00
- 8:00
- 9:00
- 10:00
- 11:00
- 12:00

CURRENT FOCUS GOALS

....
....
....
....
....
....

| TIME LEFT FOR GOALS: |

MUST DO

☐ ....
☐ ....
☐ ....

IF TIME

☐ ....
☐ ....
☐ ....

CREATIVE PLAY

....
....
....
....
....
....
....

DAILY PLANNER

RELATIONSHIPS NURTURED

....
....
....
....
....
....

TODAY'S POSITIVES

....
....
....
....
....
....

Notes

DAILY CHALLENGE
Create a music playlist to help you tap into heightened emotions.

DAILY PLANNER

TODAY'S DATE:

TODAY'S FOCUS:

Today's Events

- 12:00
- 1:00
- 2:00
- 3:00
- 4:00
- 5:00
- 6:00
- 7:00
- 8:00
- 9:00
- 10:00
- 11:00
- 12:00
- 1:00
- 2:00
- 3:00
- 4:00
- 5:00
- 6:00
- 7:00
- 8:00
- 9:00
- 10:00
- 11:00
- 12:00

CURRENT FOCUS GOALS

....
....
....
....
....
....

TIME LEFT FOR GOALS:

MUST DO

☐ ....
☐ ....
☐ ....

IF TIME

☐ ....
☐ ....
☐ ....

CREATIVE PLAY

....
....
....
....
....
....

RELATIONSHIPS NURTURED	TODAY'S POSITIVES
....	....
....	....
....	....
....	....
....	....

Notes

DAILY CHALLENGE
Reflect on your current representation status. Are you happy with your current circumstances?

 **DAILY PLANNER**

TODAY'S DATE:

TODAY'S FOCUS:

Today's Events

- 12:00
- 1:00
- 2:00
- 3:00
- 4:00
- 5:00
- 6:00
- 7:00
- 8:00
- 9:00
- 10:00
- 11:00
- 12:00
- 1:00
- 2:00
- 3:00
- 4:00
- 5:00
- 6:00
- 7:00
- 8:00
- 9:00
- 10:00
- 11:00
- 12:00

CURRENT FOCUS GOALS

TIME LEFT FOR GOALS:

MUST DO
- ☐
- ☐
- ☐

IF TIME
- ☐
- ☐
- ☐

CREATIVE PLAY

RELATIONSHIPS NURTURED

....
....
....
....
....
....

TODAY'S POSITIVES

....
....
....
....
....
....

Notes

DAILY CHALLENGE
Improvise a monologue, starting with the phrase "I want you to know…"

DAILY PLANNER

TODAY'S DATE:

TODAY'S FOCUS:

Today's Events

- 12:00
- 1:00
- 2:00
- 3:00
- 4:00
- 5:00
- 6:00
- 7:00
- 8:00
- 9:00
- 10:00
- 11:00
- 12:00
- 1:00
- 2:00
- 3:00
- 4:00
- 5:00
- 6:00
- 7:00
- 8:00
- 9:00
- 10:00
- 11:00
- 12:00

CURRENT FOCUS GOALS

TIME LEFT FOR GOALS:

MUST DO

- ☐
- ☐
- ☐

IF TIME

- ☐
- ☐
- ☐

CREATIVE PLAY

DAILY PLANNER

RELATIONSHIPS NURTURED

....

....

....

....

....

....

TODAY'S POSITIVES

....

....

....

....

....

....

Notes

DAILY CHALLENGE
List 5 places you've always wanted to visit.

DAILY PLANNER

TODAY'S DATE:

TODAY'S FOCUS:

Today's Events

- 12:00
- 1:00
- 2:00
- 3:00
- 4:00
- 5:00
- 6:00
- 7:00
- 8:00
- 9:00
- 10:00
- 11:00
- 12:00
- 1:00
- 2:00
- 3:00
- 4:00
- 5:00
- 6:00
- 7:00
- 8:00
- 9:00
- 10:00
- 11:00
- 12:00

CURRENT FOCUS GOALS

TIME LEFT FOR GOALS:

MUST DO

- [ ]
- [ ]
- [ ]

IF TIME

- [ ]
- [ ]
- [ ]

CREATIVE PLAY

DAILY PLANNER

RELATIONSHIPS NURTURED

....
....
....
....
....
....

TODAY'S POSITIVES

....
....
....
....
....
....

Notes

DAILY CHALLENGE
Call a supportive friend you haven't spoken to in a while.

DAILY PLANNER

TODAY'S DATE:	TODAY'S FOCUS:

Today's Events

- 12:00
- 1:00
- 2:00
- 3:00
- 4:00
- 5:00
- 6:00
- 7:00
- 8:00
- 9:00
- 10:00
- 11:00
- 12:00
- 1:00
- 2:00
- 3:00
- 4:00
- 5:00
- 6:00
- 7:00
- 8:00
- 9:00
- 10:00
- 11:00
- 12:00

CURRENT FOCUS GOALS

....
....
....
....
....

TIME LEFT FOR GOALS:

MUST DO

- ☐ ....
- ☐ ....
- ☐ ....

IF TIME

- ☐ ....
- ☐ ....
- ☐ ....

CREATIVE PLAY

....
....
....
....
....
....

DAILY PLANNER

RELATIONSHIPS NURTURED

....
....
....
....
....

TODAY'S POSITIVES

....
....
....
....
....

Notes

Order your new planner and keep the momentum going: Visit **bit.ly/corrielegge** or scan the QR code to order now. Use code **ACTNOW** at checkout for 20% off your next planner!

DAILY PLANNER

TODAY'S DATE:

TODAY'S FOCUS:

Today's Events

- 12:00
- 1:00
- 2:00
- 3:00
- 4:00
- 5:00
- 6:00
- 7:00
- 8:00
- 9:00
- 10:00
- 11:00
- 12:00
- 1:00
- 2:00
- 3:00
- 4:00
- 5:00
- 6:00
- 7:00
- 8:00
- 9:00
- 10:00
- 11:00
- 12:00

CURRENT FOCUS GOALS

TIME LEFT FOR GOALS:

MUST DO

- ☐ ....
- ☐ ....
- ☐ ....

IF TIME

- ☐ ....
- ☐ ....
- ☐ ....

CREATIVE PLAY

DAILY PLANNER

175

RELATIONSHIPS NURTURED

....
....
....
....
....
....

TODAY'S POSITIVES

....
....
....
....
....
....

Notes

DAILY CHALLENGE
Organize and back up old audition footage.

DAILY PLANNER

TODAY'S DATE:

TODAY'S FOCUS:

Today's Events

- 12:00
- 1:00
- 2:00
- 3:00
- 4:00
- 5:00
- 6:00
- 7:00
- 8:00
- 9:00
- 10:00
- 11:00
- 12:00
- 1:00
- 2:00
- 3:00
- 4:00
- 5:00
- 6:00
- 7:00
- 8:00
- 9:00
- 10:00
- 11:00
- 12:00

CURRENT FOCUS GOALS

....
....
....
....
....
....

TIME LEFT FOR GOALS:

MUST DO

☐ ....
☐ ....
☐ ....

IF TIME

☐ ....
☐ ....
☐ ....

CREATIVE PLAY

....
....
....
....
....
....

DAILY PLANNER

RELATIONSHIPS NURTURED

....
....
....
....
....
....

TODAY'S POSITIVES

....
....
....
....
....
....

Notes

DAILY CHALLENGE
Write a piece of fan mail for yourself. Send it.

DAILY PLANNER

TODAY'S DATE:

TODAY'S FOCUS:

Today's Events

- 12:00
- 1:00
- 2:00
- 3:00
- 4:00
- 5:00
- 6:00
- 7:00
- 8:00
- 9:00
- 10:00
- 11:00
- 12:00
- 1:00
- 2:00
- 3:00
- 4:00
- 5:00
- 6:00
- 7:00
- 8:00
- 9:00
- 10:00
- 11:00
- 12:00

CURRENT FOCUS GOALS

TIME LEFT FOR GOALS:

MUST DO
- ☐
- ☐
- ☐

IF TIME
- ☐
- ☐
- ☐

CREATIVE PLAY

RELATIONSHIPS NURTURED

....
....
....
....
....
....

TODAY'S POSITIVES

....
....
....
....
....
....

Notes

DAILY CHALLENGE
Send a message to a fellow actor you haven't spoken to in a while, just to check in.

 **DAILY PLANNER**

TODAY'S DATE:	TODAY'S FOCUS:

Today's Events

12:00
1:00
2:00
3:00
4:00
5:00
6:00
7:00
8:00
9:00
10:00
11:00
12:00
1:00
2:00
3:00
4:00
5:00
6:00
7:00
8:00
9:00
10:00
11:00
12:00

CURRENT FOCUS GOALS

....
....
....
....
....
....
....

TIME LEFT FOR GOALS:

MUST DO

☐ ....
☐ ....
☐ ....

IF TIME

☐ ....
☐ ....
☐ ....

CREATIVE PLAY

....
....
....
....
....
....
....

DAILY PLANNER

RELATIONSHIPS NURTURED

....
....
....
....
....
....

TODAY'S POSITIVES

....
....
....
....
....
....

Notes

DAILY CHALLENGE
Declutter 3 articles of clothing you never wear.

DAILY PLANNER

TODAY'S DATE:

TODAY'S FOCUS:

Today's Events

- 12:00
- 1:00
- 2:00
- 3:00
- 4:00
- 5:00
- 6:00
- 7:00
- 8:00
- 9:00
- 10:00
- 11:00
- 12:00
- 1:00
- 2:00
- 3:00
- 4:00
- 5:00
- 6:00
- 7:00
- 8:00
- 9:00
- 10:00
- 11:00
- 12:00

CURRENT FOCUS GOALS

TIME LEFT FOR GOALS:

MUST DO

- ☐
- ☐
- ☐

IF TIME

- ☐
- ☐
- ☐

CREATIVE PLAY

RELATIONSHIPS NURTURED

....
....
....
....
....
....

TODAY'S POSITIVES

....
....
....
....
....
....

Notes

DAILY CHALLENGE
Update your acting website with any recent work.

DAILY PLANNER

| TODAY'S DATE: | TODAY'S FOCUS: |

Today's Events

- 12:00
- 1:00
- 2:00
- 3:00
- 4:00
- 5:00
- 6:00
- 7:00
- 8:00
- 9:00
- 10:00
- 11:00
- 12:00
- 1:00
- 2:00
- 3:00
- 4:00
- 5:00
- 6:00
- 7:00
- 8:00
- 9:00
- 10:00
- 11:00
- 12:00

CURRENT FOCUS GOALS

....
....
....
....
....
....

| TIME LEFT FOR GOALS: |

MUST DO

☐ ....
☐ ....
☐ ....

IF TIME

☐ ....
☐ ....
☐ ....

CREATIVE PLAY

....
....
....
....
....
....

DAILY PLANNER

RELATIONSHIPS NURTURED
....
....
....
....
....
....

TODAY'S POSITIVES
....
....
....
....
....
....

Notes

DAILY CHALLENGE
Create a clear vocal warm-up routine. Commit to doing it daily for one week.

DAILY PLANNER

| TODAY'S DATE: | TODAY'S FOCUS: |

Today's Events

- 12:00
- 1:00
- 2:00
- 3:00
- 4:00
- 5:00
- 6:00
- 7:00
- 8:00
- 9:00
- 10:00
- 11:00
- 12:00
- 1:00
- 2:00
- 3:00
- 4:00
- 5:00
- 6:00
- 7:00
- 8:00
- 9:00
- 10:00
- 11:00
- 12:00

CURRENT FOCUS GOALS

....
....
....
....
....
....

TIME LEFT FOR GOALS:

MUST DO

☐ ....
☐ ....
☐ ....

IF TIME

☐ ....
☐ ....
☐ ....

CREATIVE PLAY

....
....
....
....
....
....

DAILY PLANNER

RELATIONSHIPS NURTURED

....
....
....
....
....

TODAY'S POSITIVES

....
....
....
....
....

Notes

DAILY CHALLENGE
Audit one of your casting profiles.

DAILY PLANNER

TODAY'S DATE:	TODAY'S FOCUS:

Today's Events

- 12:00
- 1:00
- 2:00
- 3:00
- 4:00
- 5:00
- 6:00
- 7:00
- 8:00
- 9:00
- 10:00
- 11:00
- 12:00
- 1:00
- 2:00
- 3:00
- 4:00
- 5:00
- 6:00
- 7:00
- 8:00
- 9:00
- 10:00
- 11:00
- 12:00

CURRENT FOCUS GOALS

....
....
....
....
....

TIME LEFT FOR GOALS:

MUST DO

☐ ....
☐ ....
☐ ....

IF TIME

☐ ....
☐ ....
☐ ....

CREATIVE PLAY

....
....
....
....
....
....

RELATIONSHIPS NURTURED

....
....
....
....
....
....

TODAY'S POSITIVES

....
....
....
....
....
....

Notes

DAILY CHALLENGE
Make a list of 10 things you used to love that you haven't done in a while. Make plans to do one of them this week.

DAILY PLANNER

TODAY'S DATE:

TODAY'S FOCUS:

Today's Events

12:00
1:00
2:00
3:00
4:00
5:00
6:00
7:00
8:00
9:00
10:00
11:00
12:00
1:00
2:00
3:00
4:00
5:00
6:00
7:00
8:00
9:00
10:00
11:00
12:00

CURRENT FOCUS GOALS

TIME LEFT FOR GOALS:

MUST DO

☐ ....
☐ ....
☐ ....

IF TIME

☐ ....
☐ ....
☐ ....

CREATIVE PLAY

RELATIONSHIPS NURTURED

....
....
....
....
....
....

TODAY'S POSITIVES

....
....
....
....
....
....

Notes

DAILY CHALLENGE
Audit your online presence—do your website and social media accounts reflect your brand?

DAILY PLANNER

TODAY'S DATE:

TODAY'S FOCUS:

Today's Events

- 12:00
- 1:00
- 2:00
- 3:00
- 4:00
- 5:00
- 6:00
- 7:00
- 8:00
- 9:00
- 10:00
- 11:00
- 12:00
- 1:00
- 2:00
- 3:00
- 4:00
- 5:00
- 6:00
- 7:00
- 8:00
- 9:00
- 10:00
- 11:00
- 12:00

CURRENT FOCUS GOALS

....
....
....
....
....
....

TIME LEFT FOR GOALS:

MUST DO

☐ ....
☐ ....
☐ ....

IF TIME

☐ ....
☐ ....
☐ ....

CREATIVE PLAY

....
....
....
....
....
....

DAILY PLANNER

RELATIONSHIPS NURTURED

....
....
....
....
....
....

TODAY'S POSITIVES

....
....
....
....
....
....

Notes

DAILY CHALLENGE
Write a letter or email to someone whose work you admire.

DAILY PLANNER

| TODAY'S DATE: | TODAY'S FOCUS: |

Today's Events

- 12:00
- 1:00
- 2:00
- 3:00
- 4:00
- 5:00
- 6:00
- 7:00
- 8:00
- 9:00
- 10:00
- 11:00
- 12:00
- 1:00
- 2:00
- 3:00
- 4:00
- 5:00
- 6:00
- 7:00
- 8:00
- 9:00
- 10:00
- 11:00
- 12:00

CURRENT FOCUS GOALS

....
....
....
....
....
....

TIME LEFT FOR GOALS:

MUST DO

☐ ....
☐ ....
☐ ....

IF TIME

☐ ....
☐ ....
☐ ....

CREATIVE PLAY

....
....
....
....
....
....
....

DAILY PLANNER

RELATIONSHIPS NURTURED
....
....
....
....
....
....

TODAY'S POSITIVES
....
....
....
....
....
....

Notes

DAILY CHALLENGE
Brainstorm 5 ways to make extra money this month.

DAILY PLANNER

| TODAY'S DATE: | TODAY'S FOCUS: |

Today's Events

- 12:00
- 1:00
- 2:00
- 3:00
- 4:00
- 5:00
- 6:00
- 7:00
- 8:00
- 9:00
- 10:00
- 11:00
- 12:00
- 1:00
- 2:00
- 3:00
- 4:00
- 5:00
- 6:00
- 7:00
- 8:00
- 9:00
- 10:00
- 11:00
- 12:00

CURRENT FOCUS GOALS

....
....
....
....
....
....

TIME LEFT FOR GOALS:

MUST DO

☐ ....
☐ ....
☐ ....

IF TIME

☐ ....
☐ ....
☐ ....

CREATIVE PLAY

....
....
....
....
....
....
....

RELATIONSHIPS NURTURED

....
....
....
....
....
....

TODAY'S POSITIVES

....
....
....
....
....
....

Notes

DAILY CHALLENGE
Doodle for 10 minutes.

DAILY PLANNER

TODAY'S DATE:	TODAY'S FOCUS:

Today's Events

- 12:00
- 1:00
- 2:00
- 3:00
- 4:00
- 5:00
- 6:00
- 7:00
- 8:00
- 9:00
- 10:00
- 11:00
- 12:00
- 1:00
- 2:00
- 3:00
- 4:00
- 5:00
- 6:00
- 7:00
- 8:00
- 9:00
- 10:00
- 11:00
- 12:00

CURRENT FOCUS GOALS

....
....
....
....
....
....

TIME LEFT FOR GOALS:

MUST DO

- ☐ ....
- ☐ ....
- ☐ ....

IF TIME

- ☐ ....
- ☐ ....
- ☐ ....

CREATIVE PLAY

....
....
....
....
....
....

RELATIONSHIPS NURTURED

....
....
....
....
....
....

TODAY'S POSITIVES

....
....
....
....
....
....

Notes

DAILY CHALLENGE
Watch a short film. What did you like about it? What didn't you like?

 **DAILY PLANNER**

TODAY'S DATE:

TODAY'S FOCUS:

Today's Events

- 12:00
- 1:00
- 2:00
- 3:00
- 4:00
- 5:00
- 6:00
- 7:00
- 8:00
- 9:00
- 10:00
- 11:00
- 12:00
- 1:00
- 2:00
- 3:00
- 4:00
- 5:00
- 6:00
- 7:00
- 8:00
- 9:00
- 10:00
- 11:00
- 12:00

CURRENT FOCUS GOALS

....
....
....
....
....
....

TIME LEFT FOR GOALS:

MUST DO

☐ ....
☐ ....
☐ ....

IF TIME

☐ ....
☐ ....
☐ ....

CREATIVE PLAY

....
....
....
....
....
....
....
....

RELATIONSHIPS NURTURED

....
....
....
....
....
....

TODAY'S POSITIVES

....
....
....
....
....
....

Notes

DAILY CHALLENGE
Run one of your favorite scenes, this time playing the opposite character.

DAILY PLANNER

TODAY'S DATE:

TODAY'S FOCUS:

Today's Events

- 12:00
- 1:00
- 2:00
- 3:00
- 4:00
- 5:00
- 6:00
- 7:00
- 8:00
- 9:00
- 10:00
- 11:00
- 12:00
- 1:00
- 2:00
- 3:00
- 4:00
- 5:00
- 6:00
- 7:00
- 8:00
- 9:00
- 10:00
- 11:00
- 12:00

CURRENT FOCUS GOALS

TIME LEFT FOR GOALS:

MUST DO
- ☐
- ☐
- ☐

IF TIME
- ☐
- ☐
- ☐

CREATIVE PLAY

RELATIONSHIPS NURTURED

....
....
....
....
....
....

TODAY'S POSITIVES

....
....
....
....
....
....

Notes

DAILY CHALLENGE
Listen to your favorite music album.

DAILY PLANNER

| TODAY'S DATE: | TODAY'S FOCUS: |

Today's Events

- 12:00
- 1:00
- 2:00
- 3:00
- 4:00
- 5:00
- 6:00
- 7:00
- 8:00
- 9:00
- 10:00
- 11:00
- 12:00
- 1:00
- 2:00
- 3:00
- 4:00
- 5:00
- 6:00
- 7:00
- 8:00
- 9:00
- 10:00
- 11:00
- 12:00

CURRENT FOCUS GOALS

....
....
....
....
....
....

TIME LEFT FOR GOALS:

MUST DO

☐ ....
☐ ....
☐ ....

IF TIME

☐ ....
☐ ....
☐ ....

CREATIVE PLAY

....
....
....
....
....
....

RELATIONSHIPS NURTURED

....
....
....
....
....
....

TODAY'S POSITIVES

....
....
....
....
....
....

Notes

DAILY CHALLENGE
Prepare a short 30-sec introduction about yourself for networking purposes.

DAILY PLANNER

TODAY'S DATE:	TODAY'S FOCUS:

Today's Events

- 12:00
- 1:00
- 2:00
- 3:00
- 4:00
- 5:00
- 6:00
- 7:00
- 8:00
- 9:00
- 10:00
- 11:00
- 12:00
- 1:00
- 2:00
- 3:00
- 4:00
- 5:00
- 6:00
- 7:00
- 8:00
- 9:00
- 10:00
- 11:00
- 12:00

CURRENT FOCUS GOALS

....
....
....
....
....
....

TIME LEFT FOR GOALS:

MUST DO

☐ ....
☐ ....
☐ ....

IF TIME

☐ ....
☐ ....
☐ ....

CREATIVE PLAY

....
....
....
....
....
....

RELATIONSHIPS NURTURED

....
....
....
....
....
....

TODAY'S POSITIVES

....
....
....
....
....
....

Notes

DAILY CHALLENGE
Buy tickets to an upcoming local theatre performance.

TODAY'S DATE:

TODAY'S FOCUS:

Today's Events

- 12:00
- 1:00
- 2:00
- 3:00
- 4:00
- 5:00
- 6:00
- 7:00
- 8:00
- 9:00
- 10:00
- 11:00
- 12:00
- 1:00
- 2:00
- 3:00
- 4:00
- 5:00
- 6:00
- 7:00
- 8:00
- 9:00
- 10:00
- 11:00
- 12:00

CURRENT FOCUS GOALS

....
....
....
....
....
....

TIME LEFT FOR GOALS:

MUST DO

☐ ....
☐ ....
☐ ....

IF TIME

☐ ....
☐ ....
☐ ....

CREATIVE PLAY

....
....
....
....
....
....

RELATIONSHIPS NURTURED

....
....
....
....
....
....

TODAY'S POSITIVES

....
....
....
....
....
....

Notes

DAILY CHALLENGE
Write down 5 recent acting wins (yes, you do have 5). Celebrate them!

DAILY PLANNER

TODAY'S DATE:		TODAY'S FOCUS:

Today's Events

- 12:00
- 1:00
- 2:00
- 3:00
- 4:00
- 5:00
- 6:00
- 7:00
- 8:00
- 9:00
- 10:00
- 11:00
- 12:00
- 1:00
- 2:00
- 3:00
- 4:00
- 5:00
- 6:00
- 7:00
- 8:00
- 9:00
- 10:00
- 11:00
- 12:00

CURRENT FOCUS GOALS

....
....
....
....
....
....

TIME LEFT FOR GOALS:

MUST DO

☐ ....
☐ ....
☐ ....

IF TIME

☐ ....
☐ ....
☐ ....

CREATIVE PLAY

....
....
....
....
....
....

DAILY PLANNER

RELATIONSHIPS NURTURED

....
....
....
....
....
....

TODAY'S POSITIVES

....
....
....
....
....
....

Notes

DAILY CHALLENGE
Find a new-to-you industry podcast and listen to one episode.

 **DAILY PLANNER**

TODAY'S DATE:	TODAY'S FOCUS:

Today's Events

- 12:00
- 1:00
- 2:00
- 3:00
- 4:00
- 5:00
- 6:00
- 7:00
- 8:00
- 9:00
- 10:00
- 11:00
- 12:00
- 1:00
- 2:00
- 3:00
- 4:00
- 5:00
- 6:00
- 7:00
- 8:00
- 9:00
- 10:00
- 11:00
- 12:00

CURRENT FOCUS GOALS

....
....
....
....
....
....

TIME LEFT FOR GOALS:

MUST DO

☐ ....
☐ ....
☐ ....

IF TIME

☐ ....
☐ ....
☐ ....

CREATIVE PLAY

....
....
....
....
....
....

RELATIONSHIPS NURTURED

....
....
....
....
....
....

TODAY'S POSITIVES

....
....
....
....
....
....

Notes

DAILY CHALLENGE
Audit your current subscriptions—are they all necessary?

DAILY PLANNER

TODAY'S DATE:

TODAY'S FOCUS:

Today's Events

- 12:00
- 1:00
- 2:00
- 3:00
- 4:00
- 5:00
- 6:00
- 7:00
- 8:00
- 9:00
- 10:00
- 11:00
- 12:00
- 1:00
- 2:00
- 3:00
- 4:00
- 5:00
- 6:00
- 7:00
- 8:00
- 9:00
- 10:00
- 11:00
- 12:00

CURRENT FOCUS GOALS

TIME LEFT FOR GOALS:

MUST DO

- ☐
- ☐
- ☐

IF TIME

- ☐
- ☐
- ☐

CREATIVE PLAY

RELATIONSHIPS NURTURED

....
....
....
....
....
....

TODAY'S POSITIVES

....
....
....
....
....
....

Notes

DAILY CHALLENGE
Turn off notifications for 3 distracting apps on your phone.

DAILY PLANNER

| TODAY'S DATE: | TODAY'S FOCUS: |

Today's Events

- 12:00
- 1:00
- 2:00
- 3:00
- 4:00
- 5:00
- 6:00
- 7:00
- 8:00
- 9:00
- 10:00
- 11:00
- 12:00
- 1:00
- 2:00
- 3:00
- 4:00
- 5:00
- 6:00
- 7:00
- 8:00
- 9:00
- 10:00
- 11:00
- 12:00

CURRENT FOCUS GOALS

....
....
....
....
....
....

| TIME LEFT FOR GOALS: |

MUST DO

☐ ....
☐ ....
☐ ....

IF TIME

☐ ....
☐ ....
☐ ....

CREATIVE PLAY

....
....
....
....
....
....

DAILY PLANNER

RELATIONSHIPS NURTURED
....
....
....
....
....
....

TODAY'S POSITIVES
....
....
....
....
....
....

Notes

DAILY CHALLENGE
Spend 10 minutes journaling about your dream role.

DAILY PLANNER

TODAY'S DATE:

TODAY'S FOCUS:

Today's Events

- 12:00
- 1:00
- 2:00
- 3:00
- 4:00
- 5:00
- 6:00
- 7:00
- 8:00
- 9:00
- 10:00
- 11:00
- 12:00
- 1:00
- 2:00
- 3:00
- 4:00
- 5:00
- 6:00
- 7:00
- 8:00
- 9:00
- 10:00
- 11:00
- 12:00

CURRENT FOCUS GOALS

TIME LEFT FOR GOALS:

MUST DO
- ☐
- ☐
- ☐

IF TIME
- ☐
- ☐
- ☐

CREATIVE PLAY

DAILY PLANNER

RELATIONSHIPS NURTURED

....
....
....
....
....
....

TODAY'S POSITIVES

....
....
....
....
....
....

Notes

DAILY CHALLENGE
Send a message to a new dream collaborator and introduce yourself.

DAILY PLANNER

TODAY'S DATE:

TODAY'S FOCUS:

Today's Events

- 12:00
- 1:00
- 2:00
- 3:00
- 4:00
- 5:00
- 6:00
- 7:00
- 8:00
- 9:00
- 10:00
- 11:00
- 12:00
- 1:00
- 2:00
- 3:00
- 4:00
- 5:00
- 6:00
- 7:00
- 8:00
- 9:00
- 10:00
- 11:00
- 12:00

CURRENT FOCUS GOALS

....
....
....
....
....
....

TIME LEFT FOR GOALS:

MUST DO

☐ ....
☐ ....
☐ ....

IF TIME

☐ ....
☐ ....
☐ ....

CREATIVE PLAY

....
....
....
....
....
....

RELATIONSHIPS NURTURED

....
....
....
....
....
....

TODAY'S POSITIVES

....
....
....
....
....
....

Notes

DAILY CHALLENGE
Write down 10 things you're grateful for.

DAILY PLANNER

TODAY'S DATE:

TODAY'S FOCUS:

Today's Events

- 12:00
- 1:00
- 2:00
- 3:00
- 4:00
- 5:00
- 6:00
- 7:00
- 8:00
- 9:00
- 10:00
- 11:00
- 12:00
- 1:00
- 2:00
- 3:00
- 4:00
- 5:00
- 6:00
- 7:00
- 8:00
- 9:00
- 10:00
- 11:00
- 12:00

CURRENT FOCUS GOALS

....
....
....
....
....
....

TIME LEFT FOR GOALS:

MUST DO

- ☐ ....
- ☐ ....
- ☐ ....

IF TIME

- ☐ ....
- ☐ ....
- ☐ ....

CREATIVE PLAY

....
....
....
....
....
....
....

RELATIONSHIPS NURTURED

....
....
....
....
....
....

TODAY'S POSITIVES

....
....
....
....
....
....

Notes

DAILY CHALLENGE
Organize your acting space—declutter and create an environment that inspires you.

DAILY PLANNER

TODAY'S DATE:

TODAY'S FOCUS:

Today's Events

- 12:00
- 1:00
- 2:00
- 3:00
- 4:00
- 5:00
- 6:00
- 7:00
- 8:00
- 9:00
- 10:00
- 11:00
- 12:00
- 1:00
- 2:00
- 3:00
- 4:00
- 5:00
- 6:00
- 7:00
- 8:00
- 9:00
- 10:00
- 11:00
- 12:00

CURRENT FOCUS GOALS

....
....
....
....
....
....

TIME LEFT FOR GOALS:

MUST DO

☐ ....
☐ ....
☐ ....

IF TIME

☐ ....
☐ ....
☐ ....

CREATIVE PLAY

....
....
....
....
....
....

RELATIONSHIPS NURTURED

....
....
....
....
....
....

TODAY'S POSITIVES

....
....
....
....
....
....

Notes

DAILY CHALLENGE
Dive into your deepest storage and find 3 unused items to part with.

DAILY PLANNER

TODAY'S DATE:

TODAY'S FOCUS:

Today's Events

12:00
1:00
2:00
3:00
4:00
5:00
6:00
7:00
8:00
9:00
10:00
11:00
12:00
1:00
2:00
3:00
4:00
5:00
6:00
7:00
8:00
9:00
10:00
11:00
12:00

CURRENT FOCUS GOALS

TIME LEFT FOR GOALS:

MUST DO
☐
☐
☐

IF TIME
☐
☐
☐

CREATIVE PLAY

RELATIONSHIPS NURTURED

....
....
....
....
....
....

TODAY'S POSITIVES

....
....
....
....
....
....

Notes

DAILY CHALLENGE
Design a specific physical warm-up routine. Commit to doing it daily for one week.

DAILY PLANNER

TODAY'S DATE:

TODAY'S FOCUS:

Today's Events

- 12:00
- 1:00
- 2:00
- 3:00
- 4:00
- 5:00
- 6:00
- 7:00
- 8:00
- 9:00
- 10:00
- 11:00
- 12:00
- 1:00
- 2:00
- 3:00
- 4:00
- 5:00
- 6:00
- 7:00
- 8:00
- 9:00
- 10:00
- 11:00
- 12:00

CURRENT FOCUS GOALS

....
....
....
....
....
....

TIME LEFT FOR GOALS:

MUST DO

☐ ....
☐ ....
☐ ....

IF TIME

☐ ....
☐ ....
☐ ....

CREATIVE PLAY

....
....
....
....
....
....
....

RELATIONSHIPS NURTURED

....
....
....
....
....
....

TODAY'S POSITIVES

....
....
....
....
....
....

Notes

DAILY CHALLENGE
Declutter your digital photos and videos. Delete duplicates or blurry images to free up space.

DAILY PLANNER

TODAY'S DATE:

TODAY'S FOCUS:

Today's Events

- 12:00
- 1:00
- 2:00
- 3:00
- 4:00
- 5:00
- 6:00
- 7:00
- 8:00
- 9:00
- 10:00
- 11:00
- 12:00
- 1:00
- 2:00
- 3:00
- 4:00
- 5:00
- 6:00
- 7:00
- 8:00
- 9:00
- 10:00
- 11:00
- 12:00

CURRENT FOCUS GOALS

TIME LEFT FOR GOALS:

MUST DO
- [ ]
- [ ]
- [ ]

IF TIME
- [ ]
- [ ]
- [ ]

CREATIVE PLAY

RELATIONSHIPS NURTURED

....
....
....
....
....
....

TODAY'S POSITIVES

....
....
....
....
....
....

Notes

DAILY CHALLENGE
Spend 10 minutes clearing out your digital files.

MY LIFE PIE NOW

Take a moment to reflect on how your life has evolved over the past 12 weeks. Shade in your current levels of fulfillment in each area in the life pie below. Then, compare this pie to your original pie. Be sure to celebrate your growth.

Use this new life pie as a guide to envision what you'd like to continue transforming in the next 12 weeks. Remember, this was only the beginning.

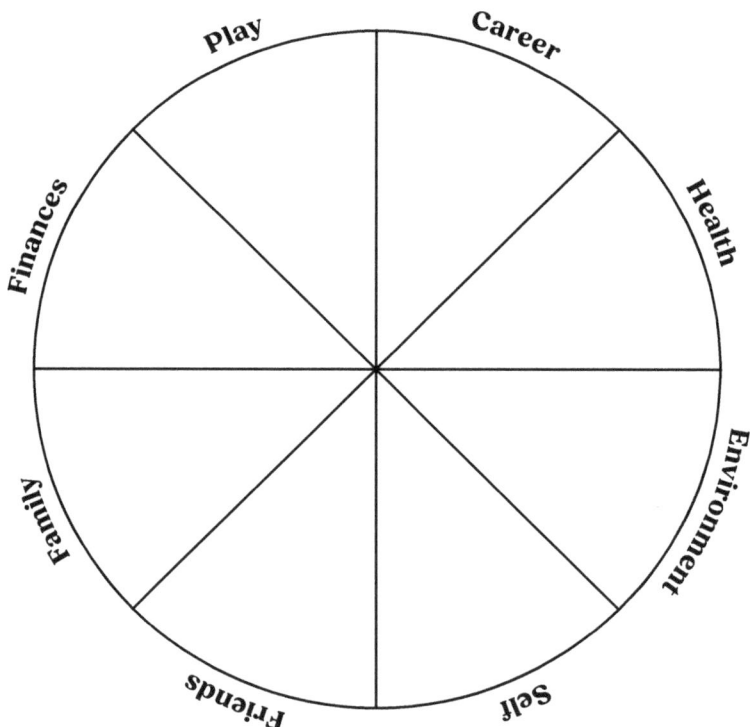

Career
WHAT'S WORKING..
....
....
AREA FOR GROWTH ....
....
....

Health
WHAT'S WORKING..
....
....
AREA FOR GROWTH ....
....
....

Environment
WHAT'S WORKING..
....
....
AREA FOR GROWTH ....
....
....

Self
WHAT'S WORKING..
....
....
AREA FOR GROWTH ....
....
....

Friends

WHAT'S WORKING ....
....
....

AREA FOR GROWTH ....
....
....

Family

WHAT'S WORKING ....
....
....

AREA FOR GROWTH ....
....
....

Finances

WHAT'S WORKING ....
....
....

AREA FOR GROWTH ....
....
....

Play

WHAT'S WORKING ....
....
....

AREA FOR GROWTH ....
....
....

Notes

MY 12-WEEK REFLECTION

Reconnect with the vision you created for your dream life. Does anything need tweaking?

Revisit your three focus goals. How far did you get with each? Did you accomplish what you set out to do?

What went well over these past 12 weeks? Is there anything you can add to your list of wins?

What didn't go as planned, didn't work, or felt challenging? Are there any lessons to be learned? ....
....
....
....
....
....
....
....
....
....

What habits or actions do you want to keep doing? What do you want to start doing? What do you want to stop doing? ....
....
....
....
....
....
....
....
....
....

How have you grown in the last 12 weeks? What led to that growth? ....
....
....
....
....
....
....
....

SET UP YOUR NEXT
THE ACTOR'S LIFE PLANNER

- ☐ Make any needed tweaks to your **LIFE PIE** and **DREAM LIFE** pages to ensure they still feel aligned with your goals. Have fun recreating them in your new planner.
- ☐ Determine your next three focus goals and make a plan to reach them.
- ☐ Fill in your monthly pages, making sure to prioritize time for the most important action items related to your focus goals.
- ☐ Revisit and update your **MINI HABITS** and **DREAM WEEK** pages so that they continue to support your vision for your dream life.

 Visit **ACTANDCREATIVES.COM/PLANNER** or scan the QR code to order your new planner, access additional resources, and more!

Want to take this one step further?
Here are three ways I can support you:

1. Follow me at **@ACTANDCREATIVES** on Instagram and YouTube.

2. Sign up for my newsletter and receive weekly insights, tips, and inspiration to help you thrive in your acting career and creative life. You'll also be the first to know about upcoming opportunities like live programs, workshops, courses, free trainings, and more. Scan the QR code or visit: **ACTANDCREATIVES.COM/NEWSLETTER**

3. Join **THE ACTOR'S PLAYGROUND**, a community of professional actors who meet for regular, coaching-free rehearsal time focused on reconnecting with the child-like joy of acting. Scan the QR code or visit: **ACTANDCREATIVES.COM/PLAYGROUND**

NOTES

NOTES

NOTES

NOTES

NOTES

NOTES

NOTES

NOTES

NOTES

NOTES